KANSAS
Cook Book

Cooking Across America
Cook Book Series™

**GOLDEN
WEST** ☼
PUBLISHERS

Acknowledgements

Kansas Wheat Commission, Manhattan, KS <kswheat.com> (pages 34 and 87)

To obtain white wheat berries, bulgur and bran, contact the American White Wheat Producers Assn., Atchison, KS (913-367-4422)

National Chicken Council <www.eatchicken.com> Sponsored by the National Chicken Council and the U. S. Poultry & Egg Assn. (page 49)

National Sunflower Assn., Bismark, ND <www.sunflowernsa.com> (pages 25, 52, 65)

Pig Out Publications Inc. (Karen Adler) <www.pigoutpublications.com> provided the following recipes: *"Nuclear" Chicken Wings* (page 10), *Congressional Pork Robusto Maduro* (page 11), *The Baron's Barbeque Chicken* (page 37), *Prize Winning Barbecued Ribs* (page 38), *Barbecued Rib Roast* and *Guy's Fuzzy Navel Steak* (page 39).

Whole Wheat Cookery: Treasures from the Wheat Bin, by Howard and Anna Ruth Beck (pages 8, 21, 26, 31)

Special thanks to Sandra Gonsher of Overland Park for her assistance with recipe compilation

For a complete listing of all Recipe Contributors see page 93

Printed in the United States of America

ISBN #1-885590-31-8

Copyright © 2000 by Golden West Publishers. All rights reserved. This book or any portion thereof, may not be reproduced in any form, except for review purposes, without the written permission of the publisher.

Information in this book is deemed to be authentic and accurate by author and publisher. However, they disclaim any liability incurred in connection with the use of information appearing in this book.

Golden West Publishers, Inc.
4113 N. Longview Ave.
Phoenix, AZ 85014, USA

(602) 265-4392
Visit our website: www.goldenwestpublishers.com

Kansas Cook Book
Table of Contents

Appetizers

Breakfast & Brunch

Soups & Salads

Main Dishes

Table of Contents (continued)

Kansas!

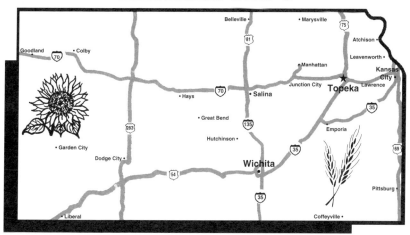

Introduction

Welcome to Kansas, known as both the Wheat State and the Sunflower State! Kansas is one of the leading agricultural states in the nation. In fact, Kansas leads the country in wheat production. *Kansas Cook Book* features many recipes utilizing wheat as a primary ingredient, including *Hearty Bulgur Salad* (page 34) and *Whole-Wheat Sugar Cookies* (page 87).

From Dodge City to Topeka and from Kansas City to Wichita, these tried and true recipes have been contributed by Kansas homemakers, with many generations of experience feeding hungry families and farmhands, by restaurants specializing in the finest Kansas cuisines, by agricultural associations (Kansas Wheat Commission, National Chicken Council) and bed & breakfasts, ranches and lodges.

Kansas has a rich pioneer spirit and heritage, which is reflected in the diverse array of tempting recipes presented in this book. Included are recipes which can trace their origins back to pioneer and "cow town" days (*Pepperloin Steak with Mustard Sauce,* page 50) and there are recipes of more recent vintage (*Baked Beans Kansas-Style,* page 46). All the recipes in the *Kansas Cook Book* are kitchen-tested family favorites which your family will love, too!

Kansas Facts

Size – 14th largest state with an area of 82,282 square miles
Population – 2,583,745 *(certified July 1997)*
State Capital – Topeka, capital since 1861
Statehood – January 29, 1861; the 34th
    state admitted to the Union
State Song – "Home on the Range"
State Nickname – The Sunflower State,
    Wheat State, Jayhawker State
    and Midway, USA

State Flower
Wild Native
Sunflower

State Motto – *Ad Astra Per Aspera*
    "To the Stars Through Difficulties"
State Animal – American Buffalo
State Insect – Honeybee
State Reptile – Ornate Box Turtle
State Amphibian – Barred Tiger
    Salamander

State Bird   **State Tree**
Western   Cottonwood
Meadowlark

Famous Kansans

Kirstie Alley, *actress;* Edward Asner,*actor;* Roscoe "Fatty" Arbuckle, *actor;* Deborah Bryant, *Miss America;* George Washington Carver, *scientist;* Clyde Cessna, *airplane manufacturer;* Wilt "The Stilt" Chamberlain,*basketball player;* Walter P. Chrysler, *auto manufacturer;* William "Buffalo Bill" Cody, *entrepreneur;* Dalton Gang, *bank robbers;* Robert Dole, *politician;* Amelia Earhart, *aviator;* Wyatt Earp, *marshal;* Dwight D. Eisenhower, *34th president of the U.S.;* Jean Harlow, *actress;* Gary Hart, *politician;* "Wild Bill" Hickok, *marshal;* Dennis Hopper, *actor;* Buster Keaton, *comedian;* Emmett Kelly, *clown;* Stan Kenton, *jazz musician;* James Lehrer, *broadcaster;* William "Bat" Masterson, *sheriff;* Mary McCarthy, *actress;* Hattie McDaniel, *actress;* Karl Menninger, *psychiatrist;* Vera Miles, *actress;* Carrie Nation, *temperance advocate;* Zazu Pitts, *actress;* Frederick Remington, *painter & sculptor;* Charles "Buddy" Rogers, *actor;* Damon Runyon, *journalist;* Marilyn Smith, *tennis player;* Rex Stout, *writer;* John Cameron Swayze, *news commentator;* Vivian Vance, *actress.*

Dill Dip in Swedish Rye

"Our state has a rich ethnic diversity. That fact is especially true in southwest Kansas where I grew up hearing many languages spoken regularly. My family and friends developed a taste for a wide variety of ethnic foods."

Kathleen Holt—Cimarron Hotel & Restaurant (est. 1886),
Cimarron

1 pkg. (10 oz.) frozen chopped SPINACH
1 cup MAYONNAISE
1/4 cup DILL WEED
1 bunch GREEN ONIONS, chopped
2 cloves GARLIC, minced
SALT and PEPPER to taste
1 ROUND SWEDISH RYE LOAF, uncut
Assorted HARD ROLLS

Thaw spinach. Place in a colander and press out all liquid. In a bowl, mix all remaining ingredients together, except bread and rolls. Add spinach and refrigerate for at least 1 hour to let flavors blend. Make a bread 'bowl' by tearing 1-inch pieces of bread from the center of the rye round; place on a large tray. Tear rolls into pieces and arrange around the bread bowl. When ready to serve, fill the bread bowl with dip.

Baked Artichoke-Spinach Dip

"Whenever I ask, 'What dip do you want?', the answer is always for this one. Even small children like it!"

Joyce M. Jandera—Hanover

1/2 cup MAYONNAISE or SALAD DRESSING
1/2 cup SOUR CREAM
1/2 cup grated PARMESAN CHEESE
3/4 cup shredded MOZZARELLA CHEESE, divided
1-2 tsp. DIJON MUSTARD
Dash WHITE PEPPER
1 can (14 oz.) ARTICHOKE HEARTS, drained and coarsely chopped
1 cup coarsely chopped SPINACH LEAVES
1/2 cup finely chopped RED ONION

In a large bowl, combine mayonnaise, sour cream, Parmesan, 1/2 cup of mozzarella, mustard and pepper. Stir in artichoke hearts, spinach and onion. Transfer mixture to a 1-quart casserole dish and cover; chill for at least 3 hours. Bake at 350° for 30-40 minutes or until thoroughly heated. Top with the remaining 1/4 cup of mozzarella. Bake 5 minutes longer or until cheese melts. Serve with bread or crackers.

Parmesan Cheese Sticks

From "Whole Wheat Cookery" by Howard & Anna Ruth Beck— Hesston

WHOLE WHEAT BREAD
BUTTER or MARGARINE, melted
1/2 cup CEREAL CRUMBS
1 1/2 oz. grated PARMESAN CHEESE
1/4 tsp. GARLIC SALT

Trim crusts from bread. Cut each slice into 4 strips. Dip strips into melted butter, then roll in mixture of crumbs, cheese and garlic salt. Place on a cookie sheet. Bake at 425° about 7 minutes.

Viva Italia!

"A simple but elegant and impressive appetizer. Great for an outdoor barbecue on a Kansas springtime evening."

Deborah Hill—Coffeyville

2 pkgs. (8 oz. ea.) CREAM CHEESE, softened
1 1/2 Tbsp. ITALIAN SEASONING
1 cup shredded MOZZARELLA CHEESE
1 EGG WHITE, beaten
1 pkg. (17 oz.) frozen PUFF PASTRY DOUGH, thawed
MARINARA SAUCE

In a bowl, blend cream cheese and Italian seasoning together; fold in mozzarella. Scoop mixture onto a large piece of plastic wrap and form into one large, flat shape. Chill for several hours until mixture is semi-firm and easy to handle. Wrap in puff pastry dough. Glaze the top with egg white and bake (per the product guidelines) until pastry is golden brown and crisp. Cut into thick wedges or slices and serve warm with marinara sauce.

 Kansas was named after the Indians that the Sioux called the Konza, meaning "people of the south wind."

Kansas Caviar

"This is a great dip for tortilla chips, toast rounds or crackers. I have served it with Italian dinners, Mexican fiestas or just included on an hors d'oeuvre table with traditional snacks. It's definitely the 'most requested recipe' I've ever prepared."

Kathleen Holt—Cimarron Hotel & Restaurant (est. 1886), Cimarron

2 cans (4.25 oz. ea.) chopped BLACK OLIVES
2 TOMATOES, chopped
1/2 bunch GREEN ONIONS, finely sliced
1 jar (8 oz.) MILD PICANTE SAUCE
1/4 cup SALAD OIL
GARLIC SALT to taste

Mix all ingredients; blend well. Chill for 24 hours.

"Nuclear" Chicken Wings

This recipe is from Scott O'Meara who is the owner of the Board Room Bar-B-Q, in Overland Park. It was originally published in "Wild About Kansas City Barbecue."

Scott O'Meara—Overland Park

5 lbs. CHICKEN WINGS (about 60)
1 1/2 cups BARBECUE SPICE
3 Tbsp. crushed RED PEPPER FLAKES
1 Tbsp. ground RED PEPPER
1 Tbsp. CHILI POWDER
1 tsp. BLACK PEPPER
BARBECUE SAUCE

Cut chicken wings at the first and second joints. Remove tips and discard. Rinse wings and drain. Put spice and peppers in a large paper or plastic bag, add the wings and shake to coat completely with seasonings. Allow wings to sit for an hour. Prepare coals, adding a combination of hickory and apple wood chips and cook wings over an indirect fire for about 1 hour. Coat wings with barbecue sauce and grill directly over coals, turning constantly, until chicken is browned and thoroughly cooked.

Serves 15-20.

Marinated Mushrooms

Diane Balanoff—Leawood

1/3 cup RED WINE VINEGAR
1/3 cup CORN OIL
2 sm. VIDALIA ONIONS, thinly sliced
1 tsp. SALT
1 tsp. dried PARSLEY
1 tsp. MUSTARD
1 Tbsp. BROWN SUGAR
3 cans (4.5 oz. ea.) MUSHROOM CROWNS, drained

In a saucepan, combine all ingredients except mushrooms. Bring to a boil. Add mushrooms; simmer 5 minutes. Chill.

Makes 2 cups.

Congressional Pork Robusto Maduro

Ardie A. Davis (a.k.a. Remus Powers, Ph.B.—that's Doctor of Barbecue Philosophy), combed the countryside in search of the best pitmasters and sauce fiends in the land. This recipe was originally published in his book "The Great BBQ Sauce Book."

Ardie A. Davis—Mission

8 EGG ROLL WRAPPERS
1/4 lb. unsalted BUTTER, melted
2 cups chopped BARBECUED PORK
1/4 tsp. CAYENNE
1/2 cup crumbled FRIED PORK RINDS

Garnish:
  1/4 cup minced WHITE ONIONS
  1/4 cup chopped RED BELL PEPPER
  1 cup TOMATO-BASED BARBECUE SAUCE
  1 cup crumbled BLUE CORN TORTILLA CHIPS

Place one egg roll wrapper on a plate and brush the exposed side of the wrapper with melted butter. Place 1/4 cup pork in a row, lengthwise, near the edge of the wrapper. Sprinkle the meat with cayenne and 2 pinches of pork rinds. Roll the wrapper in the shape of a cigar. Brush the outside of the cigar with melted butter. Repeat with balance of wrappers. Place cigars on a cookie sheet and bake in a preheated oven at 325° for 20 minutes or until golden brown. Serve on a white plate. Garnish with minced onion and bell pepper. Fill a plastic squeeze bottle with the barbecue sauce and paint a striped pattern across the cigars. Circle the edge of the plate with tortilla chips.

Serves 4.

Barbecue Tips

Dry seasonings are rubbed on before grilling; marinades are used before and during cooking; sauces are brushed on just before cooking is completed or served on the side.

Cheesy Biscuit Snacks

"This is a great make-ahead recipe, perfect for appetizers or a hostess gift."

Tina Woolley—Smoky Valley Bed & Breakfast, Lindsborg

2 cups BUTTER, softened	4 cups sifted FLOUR
5 oz. PARMESAN CHEESE, grated	3 tsp. SALT
1 lb. SHARP CHEDDAR CHEESE, grated	1/2 tsp. CAYENNE
	FINE SUGAR

Preheat oven to 325°. In a bowl, cream the butter and Parmesan well, slowly adding the cheddar cheese. Add the remaining ingredients, except the sugar, and knead until fully blended to pie dough consistency. Chill the dough for 30-45 minutes. Divide dough into 4 (6-inch) pieces; roll to 1/4-inch thickness on a floured surface. Cut out biscuits and place on an ungreased cookie sheet. Bake at 325° for 12 minutes. Remove and place on a wire rack to cool. When cool, sprinkle lightly with fine sugar. Store in an airtight container.

The Lyons' House Baked Gouda

"This is our guests' favorite appetizer."

Pat Lyons—The Lyons' House Bed & Breakfast, Fort Scott

1 pkg. (8 oz.) PILLSBURY® CRESCENT ROLLS	1 tsp. DIJON MUSTARD
1 pkg. (4 oz.) GOUDA CHEESE	CREAM
	SESAME SEEDS

Preheat oven to 375°. On a cookie sheet, unroll crescent roll dough without separating rolls. Flatten half of the dough and pinch edges together. Spread with 1/2 teaspoon mustard and place the whole gouda (wax-peeled) in the center. Spread remaining mustard on the other flattened half of dough and lay it, mustard side down, on top of the cheese. Pinch edges to seal. Brush top with cream and sprinkle with sesame seeds. Bake for 15 minutes. Cut into squares; serve warm.

Apricot-Almond Coffee Cake

*"This coffee cake is nicely flavored
and delicious for breakfast."*

Mary Reese—Creek Side Farm, Fowler

2 sticks BUTTER, softened
2 cups SUGAR
2 EGGS
1 cup SOUR CREAM
1 tsp. ALMOND EXTRACT
2 cups FLOUR

1 tsp. BAKING POWDER
1/4 tsp. SALT
1 cup sliced ALMONDS
1 jar (10 oz.) APRICOT
   PRESERVES

In a large bowl, cream butter and sugar until fluffy. Beat in eggs one at a time. Fold in sour cream and almond extract. In another bowl, sift together the flour, baking powder and salt; fold into butter mixture. Place 1/3 of the mixture in a greased and floured Bundt pan. Sprinkle with 1/2 cup of the almonds and dot with 1/2 of the preserves. Next, spread the remaining batter then spoon the last of the preserves over top, finishing with the remainder of almonds. Bake at 350° for 1 hour or until done. Cool on a rack.

Cranberry-Glazed Canadian Bacon

"This is a great breakfast to serve to special guests!"

Leon "Butch" Cuppet—Savonburg

10 slices CANADIAN BACON, cut 1/4-inch thick
1 Tbsp. grated ORANGE PEEL
1/2 tsp. SUGAR
1/8 tsp. ground CLOVES
Dash of NUTMEG
1 cup WHOLE CRANBERRY SAUCE

Arrange bacon slices in an 8 x 12 baking dish. In a bowl, combine orange peel, sugar, cloves and nutmeg. Sprinkle mixture over bacon slices. Spread cranberry sauce over the top. Bake, uncovered, at 350° for 25 minutes. Serve with sauce spooned over the bacon.

Serves 5.

Pruttles

"This is an old German dish that was made on butchering day. This version is a treat we serve for breakfast with eggs and pancakes at every family reunion."

Marion Bogart—Kensington

6 lbs. PORK SHOULDER   **3 cups OATMEAL**
2 lbs. BEEF CHUCK ROAST   **SALT and PEPPER to taste**

In a large kettle, cover meat with water and boil until very tender and meat falls from the bones. Remove meat from broth; debone, grind and set aside. Strain broth. Measure 2 quarts of strained broth; return to kettle and bring to a boil. Add oatmeal. Stir constantly until oatmeal is done. Add ground meat, salt and pepper and bring to a boil. Pour mixture into loaf pans; cool until firm. When ready to serve, slice and brown in a skillet.

Golden Egg Bake

"I often serve this wonderful casserole with baked pork chops and homemade bread to my guests. It's one of their favorites!"

Novena Newman—Country Reflections Bed & Breakfast, Holton

1/2 cup sliced MUSHROOMS
1/2 cup chopped GREEN BELL PEPPER
1/4 cup BUTTER
10 EGGS
1/2 cup FLOUR
1 tsp. BAKING POWDER
16 oz. COTTAGE CHEESE
16 oz. COLBY-JACK CHEESE, shredded
8 oz. SAUSAGE, cooked and crumbled
6 slices BACON, cooked and crumbled
1 can (4 oz.) sliced BLACK OLIVES

In a skillet, sauté mushrooms and bell pepper in butter. In a bowl, combine eggs, flour and baking powder; mix well. Add mushroom mixture, cheeses, sausage and bacon; stir. Pour mixture into a lightly buttered 9 x 13 baking dish. Top with olives. Bake, uncovered, at 400° for 15 minutes; reduce temperature to 350° and bake for 25-35 minutes longer.

Serves 12.

Mom's Pear Honey

"When I was a child I loved to spend time with my grandmother in her kitchen. I called her 'mom'. She cooked and baked wonderful foods, including this delicious pear honey."

Lawanda J. Gorton—Ottawa

5 lbs. PEARS, peeled, cored and coarsely ground
10 cups SUGAR
2 cans (8.5 oz. ea.) crushed PINEAPPLE

Place all ingredients in a large saucepan. Bring to a boil while stirring constantly and cook until the mixture is thick and pears are clear. Pour into hot, sterilized jars and seal. Use as a spread on hot muffins, bread or biscuits.

Yields 7 pints.

French Bread Breakfast

"A favorite family breakfast made the night before and ready to pop in the oven early on a holiday morning."

Maralee Thompson—Lansing

1 1/2 cups packed BROWN SUGAR
3/4 cup BUTTER
1/4 cup + 2 Tbsp. LIGHT CORN SYRUP
10 (1 3/4-inch thick) slices FRENCH BREAD
4 EGGS, beaten
2 1/2 cups MILK or HALF and HALF
1 Tbsp. VANILLA
1/4 tsp. SALT
1 1/2 tsp. CINNAMON
3 Tbsp. SUGAR
1/4 cup BUTTER, melted

Combine brown sugar, butter and corn syrup in a saucepan. Cook and stir for 5 minutes or until bubbling. Remove from heat and pour into a greased 9 x 13 baking dish. Layer slices of bread on top of mixture. In a bowl, combine eggs with milk, vanilla and salt; stir well. Pour mixture over bread. Cover and chill for 8 hours. Before cooking, combine cinnamon and sugar in a bowl; sprinkle mixture over bread then drizzle melted butter over top. Bake, uncovered, at 350° for 45 minutes.

Serves 4-6.

About Kansas

The terrain and climate of Kansas are quite diverse. From the arid, near-desert southwest with its cactus, sagebrush and yucca, to the rolling woodlands of eastern Kansas, the state provides a wide variety of plant life and geographic forms. Kansas is dominated by the central Flint Hills where large tracts of unplowed tall grass are found. The Tallgrass Prairie Preserve's 11,000 acres are the largest protected tall grass prairie in the United States. Second largest is the Konza Prairie's 8,600 acres.

Sally's Sausage Fondue

"This is a nice brunch recipe that can be prepared ahead of time. It was given to me by my friend, Sally."

Twila Pearson—Hoxie

8 slices of BREAD, cubed
2 cups shredded SHARP CHEESE
1 1/2 lbs. LINK SAUSAGE
4 EGGS, beaten
2 1/4 cups MILK

3/4 tsp. DRY MUSTARD
1 can (10.75 oz.) CREAM OF
   MUSHROOM SOUP
1/2 cup MILK

Place bread in a greased 8 x 12 baking dish; top with cheese. Cut sausage links into thirds, place in a skillet and brown. Drain and place on top of cheese. Blend eggs, milk and mustard in a bowl, then pour over sausage. Cover and refrigerate overnight. When ready to cook, blend soup and milk in a bowl; pour over bread mixture. Cook at 300° for 1 1/2 hours.

Serves 12.

Breakfast Casserole

"Our guests love this and I have given the recipe to many of them."

Lola Ediger—The Wrought Iron Inn Bed & Breakfast, Hutchinson

1 pkg. (16 oz.) frozen HASH BROWN POTATOES
1 lb. BULK SAUSAGE, cooked and crumbled
6 EGGS
1 1/2 cups MILK
1 tsp. SALT
1 tsp. DRY MUSTARD
1 1/2 cups shredded CHEDDAR CHEESE

Grease a 9 x 13 glass baking dish. Spread hash browns in dish; sprinkle with sausage. In a bowl, beat eggs and milk together. Add salt, dry mustard and cheese; mix well. Pour egg mixture over sausage. Refrigerate overnight. Bake at 350° for 45 minutes or until a knife inserted into center comes out clean.

Serves 6-8.

Mom Flory's Mush Cakes

"My mother, 'Mom Flory', serves these mush cakes to our family for breakfast every Memorial Day. We enjoy them with eggs, biscuits, sausage gravy or hot sorghum."

Lawanda J. Gorton—Ottawa

5 cups WATER
1 cup MILK

2 1/2 tsp. SALT
2 cups CORNMEAL

In a saucepan, bring 4 cups of water to a boil. In a bowl, mix milk, salt, cornmeal and remaining water. Pour this mixture into the boiling water. Cook slowly until mixture thickens. Pour into a buttered loaf pan. When cool, cover with plastic wrap and refrigerate overnight until ready to use. To serve, slice into 1/4-inch thick slices. Fry in butter or shortening until golden brown on both sides.

Serves 6-8.

Did You Know?
The first woman mayor in the United States, Susanna Salter, was elected to office in Argonia in 1887.

German Baked Eggs

"This is a variation of an egg dish that was made by my German ancestors who settled in the middle of Kansas in the late 1800s. Most of them were farmers and produced their own milk, eggs and cheeses."

Barbara Stoecklein—Plumb House Bed & Breakfast, Emporia

12 EGGS
1 lb. MONTEREY JACK
   CHEESE, shredded
2 cups COTTAGE CHEESE

1/4 cup FLOUR
1 tsp. DRY MUSTARD
1 tsp. BAKING POWDER
1/4 lb. MARGARINE, melted

In a large bowl, beat eggs; mix in cheeses, flour, dry mustard and baking powder. Add the margarine and stir until blended. Pour mixture into a buttered 9 x 13 baking dish and bake at 350° for 35 minutes or until eggs are cooked and top is golden brown.

Serves 6.

Caramel Pecan Rolls

"The flour we use in this recipe is milled just south of us at Hudson. It is a favorite breakfast treat for all of our guests."

R. Dale and Doris J. Nitzel—Peaceful Acres Bed & Breakfast,
Great Bend

Dough:
- 1 pkg. ACTIVE DRY YEAST
- 1 cup warm WATER
- 1/4 cup SUGAR
- 1 tsp. SALT
- 2 Tbsp. MARGARINE, softened
- 1 EGG
- 3 1/4-3 1/2 cups FLOUR

1/2 cup SUGAR
2 tsp. CINNAMON
1/3 cup MARGARINE, melted
1 Tbsp. CORN SYRUP
1/2 cup packed BROWN SUGAR
2/3 cup PECAN HALVES

In a large bowl, dissolve yeast in warm water. Add sugar, salt, margarine, egg and 2 cups of the flour; beat until smooth. With spoon or hand, work in enough of the remaining flour until dough is easy to handle. Place in a greased bowl, lightly grease top and cover tightly. Let rise in a warm place; punch down. Let rise again. Place dough on a floured surface and pat into a rectangular shape. Mix sugar and cinnamon together. Brush dough with melted margarine and sprinkle with cinnamon-sugar mixture. Roll dough by hand into an 18-inch log; slice into 1-inch pieces. Combine corn syrup, brown sugar and pecans; spread in bottom of a baking pan. Place dough slices on top of the mixture; let rise. Bake at 350° for 30 minutes or until golden brown. To serve, invert onto a large platter. This recipe can be made ahead of time, refrigerated overnight and baked in the morning.

Yields 18 rolls.

Sour Cream Coffee Cake

"I have used this recipe for 20 years."

Joan Donahue—Clover Cliff Bed 'N Breakfast, Inc., Elmdale

Coffeecake:
- 1 cup BUTTER, softened
- 1 cup SUGAR
- 3 EGGS, beaten
- 1 tsp. VANILLA
- 2 1/2 cups sifted FLOUR
- 2 tsp. BAKING POWDER
- 1 tsp. BAKING SODA
- 1/2 tsp. SALT
- 1 cup SOUR CREAM

Topping:
- 3/4 cup packed BROWN SUGAR
- 1/2 cup chopped PECANS
- 2 tsp. CINNAMON

In a bowl, cream butter and sugar, then mix in eggs and vanilla. In another bowl, combine dry ingredients; add to butter mixture alternately with sour cream. Pour half of the batter into a greased 9 x 13 pan or two 8 x 8 pans. In a small bowl, mix topping ingredients; sprinkle 1/3 of the topping over the batter. Top with remaining batter and sprinkle with the last 2/3 of the topping. Bake at 375° for 30 minutes in 9 x 13 pan; 45 minutes if using 8 x 8 pans.

Serves 8-12.

Oatmeal Pancakes

Merry Barker—Flint Hills Bed & Breakfast, Council Grove

- 1 1/2 cups QUICK OATS
- 2 cups BUTTERMILK
- 2 EGGS, beaten
- 3/4 cup FLOUR
- 1 tsp. SUGAR
- 2/3 tsp. SALT
- 2 tsp. BAKING SODA

Pour oats into a mixing bowl; blend in buttermilk and eggs. In a separate bowl, combine all remaining ingredients; add to buttermilk mixture. Cook on a hot griddle until golden brown. These are thick and will take a little longer to cook than regular pancakes. Serve with warm syrup or fruit jam.

Serves 6.

Sugarless Waffles with Sugarless Syrup

Elaine Clark—Wellington

3 EGGS, separated
1 cup MILK
1/2 cup COOKING OIL
1/2 tsp. SALT

1 cup FINE WHOLE-WHEAT
  FLOUR
2 tsp. BAKING POWDER

Place egg yolks, milk and oil in blender; blend until smooth. Combine salt, flour and baking powder in a bowl and add to blended mixture. In a mixing bowl, beat egg whites until stiff; gently fold egg yolk mixture into the beaten egg whites. Bake in a hot waffle iron. Serve with *Sugarless Syrup.*

Sugarless Syrup

2 Tbsp. CORNSTARCH
1/4 tsp. CINNAMON (optional)

1 can (12 oz.) frozen FRUIT JUICE
1 can (12 oz.) WATER

In a saucepan, combine cornstarch, cinnamon and a small amount of fruit juice (your choice). Gradually add remaining juice and water, stirring to remove lumps. Simmer until slightly thickened.

Oatmeal Muffins

From "Whole Wheat Cookery" by Howard & Anna Ruth Beck—
Hesston

1 cup STONE GROUND
  WHOLE-WHEAT FLOUR
1/4 cup packed BROWN SUGAR
3 tsp. BAKING POWDER
1/2 tsp. SALT

6 Tbsp. SHORTENING
1 cup uncooked OATMEAL
1 EGG, beaten
1 cup MILK

Sift first four ingredients together; cut in shortening. Add oatmeal, egg and milk. Stir only until mixed. Pour into muffin cups and sprinkle with a mixture of **1/3 cup BROWN SUGAR, 1 Tbsp. FLOUR, 2 tsp. CINNAMON** and **1 Tbsp. melted BUTTER.** Bake at 425° for 15-20 minutes.

The LandMark's Scandinavian Breakfast Roll-Ups

"If available, use the traditional Swedish lingonberries in place of the raspberries."

Gary Anderson—LandMark Inn at the Historic Bank of Oberlin, Oberlin

Swedish Pancakes:

3 EGGS, beaten	3 Tbsp. SUGAR
2 cups MILK	1/2 tsp. SALT
2 Tbsp. BUTTER, melted	HAM, thinly sliced
1 1/2 cups FLOUR	

In a bowl, combine eggs, milk and butter. Beat in flour, sugar and salt. Pour 1/4 cup of the pancake batter into a small, lightly greased skillet, lifting and swirling batter evenly over the bottom of the pan. Cook on both sides until lightly browned. Lay a pancake on a plate and place a slice of ham on top. Spoon a thin layer of the *Cheese Sauce* over the ham; roll up the pancake. Place two pancakes on each serving plate and top with *Raspberry Maple Syrup*. Garnish with whipped cream and fresh raspberries.

Cheese Sauce

1/3 cup grated MEDIUM-SHARP CHEDDAR CHEESE	1/4 cup grated SWISS CHEESE
	1/2 cup SOUR CREAM

In a saucepan, combine cheeses and sour cream; heat on low heat until melted and smooth. Keep warm.

Raspberry Maple Syrup

1/2 cup LIGHT CORN SYRUP	1/2 Tbsp. BUTTER
1/2 cup packed BROWN SUGAR	1/3 cup fresh or frozen
1/4 cup WATER	RASPBERRIES (with juice)
Dash MAPLE EXTRACT	

Heat corn syrup, brown sugar and water over medium heat until sugar dissolves. Add maple extract and butter; remove from heat. Cool slightly then add raspberries.

Pumpkin Dumplin's with Apple Chutney

"A truly 'historical' recipe that our guests love."

Pat Lyons—The Lyons' House Bed & Breakfast, Fort Scott

1 can (15 oz.) PUMPKIN	1 Tbsp. ALLSPICE
1 can FLOUR	2 tsp. BAKING POWDER
1 can SUGAR	Pinch of SALT
2 EGGS, beaten	2 Tbsp. VEGETABLE OIL
1 Tbsp. CINNAMON	2 Tbsp. BUTTER

Use pumpkin can to measure flour and sugar. In a bowl, combine pumpkin, flour and sugar together. Add the next five ingredients; mix well. Heat an electric skillet to 325°; add oil and butter. Carefully drop individual tablespoons of batter into skillet and cook until brown on each side. Serve with warm *Apple Chutney*.

Apple Chutney

3 GRANNY SMITH APPLES, unpeeled, chopped	1 tsp. CINNAMON
1/4 cup APPLE or ORANGE JUICE	2 Tbsp. SUGAR

In a medium saucepan, combine ingredients. Cover and cook gently until apples are tender.

Kansas "Cow Towns"

After the Civil War, the expansion of the rail system to Kansas increased the stream of immigrants who were lured by offers of cheap land. By 1870, many small towns had sprung up. These "cow towns," such as Dodge City, Abilene, Caldwell, Newton and Wichita, took their turns as the Queens of the Trail. To this day, the cattle industry remains an important part of the state's economy.

Rose's Coffee Cake

*"This is my own recipe. I am 74 years old
and still love to bake."*

Rose Schukman—Hays

1 pkg. (14 oz.) HOT ROLL MIX
1 pkg. BETTY CROCKER® SUPER MOIST YELLOW
　　CAKE MIX WITH PUDDING
1 1/2 cups hot WATER
4 tsp. MARGARINE
1 pkg. ACTIVE DRY YEAST
4 EGGS, well-beaten
1 can (21 oz.) FRUIT PIE FILLING of choice

In a large bowl, sift the roll mix and cake mix together and set aside. In another large bowl, mix the hot water and margarine, stir and cool to lukewarm. Add the yeast package from the roll mix plus the additional yeast package; stir until dissolved. Add eggs and mix well. Gradually blend in the dry mixture. Knead well and form into a ball. Place dough in a bowl, cover with a cloth and let rise until double in bulk. Grease four 9 x 13 baking pans. Divide dough into four portions and arrange in a layer in each pan. Pour pie filling over the dough. Sprinkle **Crumb Topping** over the top; let rise. Bake at 350° for 25 minutes.

Crumb Topping

3 cups ALL-PURPOSE FLOUR
1 cup SUGAR or POWDERED SUGAR
3/4 cup MARGARINE, softened

Combine flour and sugar. Add margarine and cut into mixture using a pastry cutter or fork until it forms fine crumbs.

Did You Know?

The introduction of Turkey Red Winter Wheat by Mennonites from Russia in 1874 was a milestone in Kansas agriculture. The wheat was ideally suited to the Kansas climate and has made Kansas one of the leading wheat-producing states in the nation.

Soups
&
Salads

Sunflower Salad

National Sunflower Association

3 cups shredded CABBAGE
1 pkg. BEEF RAMEN NOODLES, broken into pieces
1/3 cup chopped ONION
1 lg. TOMATO, chopped
2 Tbsp. BACON BITS
1/4 cup SUNFLOWER KERNELS, roasted, no salt
1/4 cup shredded CHEDDAR CHEESE

Boil ramen noodles for 3-4 minutes. Drain and rinse with cold water. Refrigerate until cool. Combine all salad ingredients in a large bowl. Add *Sunflower Dressing* and refrigerate again before serving.

Sunflower Dressing

1/4 cup SUGAR
3 Tbsp. SUNFLOWER OIL
1 1/2 Tbsp. VINEGAR

1 BEEF SEASONING PACKET
(from RAMEN NOODLES)

Combine all ingredients thoroughly.

Serves 4.

Italian Sausage Soup

"A hearty soup that friends and family never stop raving about."

Marilyn Gordon—Topeka

1 1/2 cups coarsely chopped ONION
1 1/2 cups coarsely chopped CELERY
1 clove GARLIC, finely diced
3 Tbsp. OLIVE OIL
1 cup TOMATO PURÉE
1 1/4 lbs. ITALIAN SAUSAGE, sautéed
2 cups diced TOMATOES or 1 can (14 oz.) diced TOMATOES
1 can (15.5 oz.) NORTHERN BEANS
6 cups CHICKEN BROTH
1/2 tsp. OREGANO
1/2 tsp. BASIL
2 BAY LEAVES
1/8 tsp. THYME
1 tsp. CHILI POWDER
1/2 cup chopped fresh PARSLEY
3 Tbsp. SUGAR
1 cup uncooked PASTA

In a large soup kettle, sauté onion, celery and garlic in oil until barely tender. Add tomato purée and sausage; cook for 10 minutes. Mix in remaining ingredients, except pasta; simmer 30 minutes. Remove bay leaves. Add pasta and cook until it is tender. Serve with freshly grated Parmesan cheese, if desired.

Serves 10-12.

Carrot & Pineapple Salad

From "Whole Wheat Cookery" by Howard & Anna Ruth Beck—Hesston

2 1/2 cups CARROTS, shredded
1 can (8 oz.) crushed
   PINEAPPLE, drained

2 cups cooked WHOLE-WHEAT
   KERNELS
1/2 cup SALAD DRESSING

Combine all ingredients and chill.

Honey-Mustard Salad Dressing

"I enjoyed this dressing when I dined at The Pantry restaurant in Topeka. The manager was kind enough to share the recipe and gave me permission to submit it for the Kansas Cook Book."

Sandy Lundgren—Olathe

3 Tbsp. CIDER VINEGAR
3 Tbsp. HONEY
6 Tbsp. MAYONNAISE or SALAD DRESSING
1 Tbsp. finely minced ONION
1 1/2 Tbsp. chopped fresh PARSLEY
1 Tbsp. DIJON MUSTARD
Pinch of SEASONED SALT
3/4 cup VEGETABLE OIL

In a saucepan, heat the vinegar and honey; cool. In a bowl, combine all ingredients, except oil, and mix well. Slowly add oil to ingredients and blend. This is an excellent dressing on mixed spring greens.

Yields 1 1/4 cups.

Wichita

In 1864, Jesse Chisholm and James Mead established a trading post at the confluence of the Big and Little Arkansas rivers. Their trading post, on what became known as the "Chisholm Trail," was the nucleus of a settlement that built hotels and the First and Last Chance Saloon. Wichita grew, then boomed when the railroad reached it in 1872. Today, Wichita is the state's largest city with milling, meatpacking, oil production and refining and the manufacture of military and personal aircraft among the many big businesses to be found here.

Grandma's Special Bean Soup

"This is a hearty family favorite."

Jacki Cahill—Lansing

1 lb. GROUND BEEF
2 Tbsp. OLIVE OIL
1 ONION, diced
2-3 stalks CELERY, diced
2 GREEN BELL PEPPERS, diced
1 Tbsp. minced GARLIC
7 cups WATER
3 BOUILLON CUBES

2 cans (15 oz. ea.) DARK
   RED KIDNEY BEANS
1 can (16 oz.) diced
   TOMATOES
1 bag (16 oz.) frozen
   MIXED VEGETABLES
1 cup uncooked ELBOW
   MACARONI

In a large skillet, brown beef lightly in oil; add onion, celery, bell pepper and garlic and sauté. Pour mixture into a large soup kettle; add water, bouillon cubes, beans, tomatoes, vegetables and macaroni; cook until macaroni is done. Season to taste.

Serves 6.

Hearty Lentil Soup

"This is a stew-like soup. Served with crackers or breadsticks, it makes a hearty supper."

Margaret Gaskell—Horton

1 lb. GROUND BEEF
1 tsp. ONION SALT
1 can (8 oz.) TOMATO SAUCE
1 can (12 oz.) V-8® JUICE
2 cups WATER

1 cup dry LENTILS, sorted
   and washed
1 lg. POTATO, diced
1 can (15.25 oz.) CORN,
   drained

In a large skillet, brown beef seasoned with onion salt. Add tomato sauce, V-8 juice, water and lentils; simmer 1 hour. Then add potatoes and corn; continue to simmer until potatoes are tender. Season to taste. Serve with corn chips and shredded cheddar, colby or Monterey Jack cheese.

Serves 4-6.

Russo-German Sour Cream Soup & Dumplings

"This is a recipe from my mother-in-law whose ancestors were of Russian and German heritage. Many of these people, known as 'Russo-Germans', settled in western Kansas years ago."

Midge Befort—Kansas City

10 cups cold WATER
5 med. POTATOES, cut into small slices
1 lg. ONION, chopped
SALT and PEPPER to taste
2 or 3 BAY LEAVES
1/2 stick BUTTER or MARGARINE
8 oz. SOUR CREAM

In a 6-quart pot, combine water, potatoes, onion, salt, pepper and bay leaves. Bring to a boil and cook for 15 minutes or until potatoes are tender; stir occasionally. Carefully drop **Dumplings** by 1/2 teaspoonfuls into boiling mixture. Cover and let simmer for 15 minutes; turn off heat. Remove bay leaves. Add butter, stirring until melted. Add sour cream and stir until blended.

Serves 12.

Dumplings

3 EGGS
1/2 cup + 6 Tbsp. FLOUR

1 Tbsp. MILK
1/2 tsp. SALT

In a medium mixing bowl, beat eggs. Add 1/2 cup flour and beat until smooth. Add the remaining flour, milk and salt and beat until smooth.

Kansas Wheat

Kansas produces about one-fifth of all U.S. wheat. That amounts to 2 percent of the world's wheat production. In world wheat trade, Kansas is responsible for double the amount it produces—nearly 5 percent of the wheat traded in the world comes from Kansas.

Potato Soup

"This soup is a hearty favorite of my family and friends."

Sandy Lundgren—Olathe

4 lg. POTATOES, diced
1 cup chopped ONION
2 cups chopped CELERY
1/2 lb. BULK SAUSAGE or 1 pkg. (8 oz.) SAUSAGE LINKS
2 cans (12 oz. ea.) EVAPORATED MILK
2 cans (10.75 oz. ea.) CREAM OF MUSHROOM SOUP
8 oz. VELVEETA®, cubed

In a large saucepan, place potatoes, onion and celery; cover with water and simmer until tender. In a skillet, brown sausage (if using links, cut into bite-size pieces); add to vegetables. Mix in milk and soup; cook over low heat for 1 hour. Add Velveeta and heat through before serving.

Serves 6-8.

Linda's Low-Calorie Pasta Salad

Linda Zack—Leawood

1 Tbsp. OLIVE OIL
1 Tbsp. minced fresh GARLIC
5 cups diced fresh TOMATOES
1/2 tsp. BASIL
1 lb. BOW-TIE PASTA, cooked
3/4 cup CHICKEN BROTH
1/4 cup grated PARMESAN CHEESE
CAYENNE to taste

Spray a large skillet with cooking spray. Heat oil, add garlic and cook over medium heat for 1 minute. Add tomatoes and basil; cook for 3 minutes. Mix in pasta, broth, Parmesan and cayenne. Place in a serving dish, cover and chill.

Serves 8-12.

The Frozen Salad

"This has been a favorite of mine for 50 years! I especially like this salad because it travels well to parties and does not thaw quickly."

Anna K. Petrik—Wind, Earth and Sky, Caldwell

1 ctn. (8 oz.) frozen WHIPPED TOPPING, thawed
2/3 cup FAT FREE SALAD DRESSING
1 pkg. (8 oz.) MINIATURE MARSHMALLOWS
1 can (16 oz.) DARK SWEET CHERRIES, drained
1 can (8 oz.) crushed PINEAPPLE, drained
3 or 4 BANANAS, sliced
1/2 cup finely chopped PECANS or WALNUTS
STRAWBERRIES, sliced or whole
LETTUCE LEAVES

In a large mixing bowl combine whipped topping and salad dressing; stir well. Add marshmallows and let stand until the marshmallows are softened. Fold in cherries, pineapple, bananas and nuts. Press into a glass serving dish and freeze until firm; garnish with strawberries . Remove from freezer at least 10 minutes before serving. Arrange on lettuce leaves to serve.

Serves 6-8.

Waldorf with Wheat

From "Whole Wheat Cookery" by Howard & Anna Ruth Beck—Hesston

2 Tbsp. MAYONNAISE or
  SALAD DRESSING
1/2 cup PLAIN YOGURT
1/4 tsp. VANILLA
1/8 tsp. SALT

1 cup cooked WHEAT KERNELS
1/2 cup thinly sliced CELERY
2 med. APPLES, cored and sliced
WALNUT PIECES

Stir together the dressing, yogurt, vanilla and salt. Add the wheat and celery; chill, covered, until ready to serve. Stir in apples and nuts just before serving.

Serves 4.

Hot Potato Salad

"Hot potato salad is a typical German dish. We love this traditional salad."

Charlene M. Wagner—Easton

1/2 cup VINEGAR
1 cup SOUR CREAM
1/2 cup crumbled, cooked BACON
6 cups diced, boiled POTATOES

4 HARD-BOILED EGGS,
    sliced
Chopped ONION to taste
SALT and PEPPER to taste

In a large skillet, mix vinegar, sour cream and bacon and heat. Add potatoes, eggs, onion, salt and pepper. Add a small amount of sugar if too tart. Serve hot.

Serves 6-8.

Grandma Jessie's Blueberry Salad

"This purple salad recipe was created by my great-grandmother, Jessie (Young) Enders, whose father was one of the first newspaper editors in Kansas. It has been a big hit at all of our holiday dinners for as long as some in our family can remember."

Laura K. Hicks—Lansing

2 sm. boxes (3 oz. ea.) BLACK RASPBERRY or
    BLACK CHERRY GELATIN
2 cups boiling WATER
1 can (8 oz.) crushed PINEAPPLE
1 can (20 oz.) BLUEBERRIES, drained
1 pkg. (16 oz.) frozen WHIPPED TOPPING, thawed

Dissolve gelatin in boiling water. Drain pineapple, reserving juice. Add 2 cups of juice to the gelatin and stir well. Measure out 3/4 cup of mixture and set aside to gel. In a serving dish, stir pineapple and blueberries into remaining gelatin and chill until set. Blend whipped topping with the 3/4 cup of gelatin mixture and spread on top of the salad. Chill until ready to serve.

Serves 6-8.

Popeye Salad with Bacon-Vinaigrette Dressing

"My daughter made this recipe for one of our Christmas dinners. Everyone enjoyed it!"

Joyce M. Jandera—Hanover

12 oz. fresh SPINACH, torn into small pieces
1 cup sliced fresh MUSHROOMS
1/2 cup quartered CHERRY TOMATOES
4 oz. FETA CHEESE, crumbled
1 cup CROUTONS

Toss all ingredients together and chill thoroughly. Just before serving, pour the ***Bacon-Vinaigrette Dressing*** over salad and toss again. Serve immediately.

Bacon-Vinaigrette Dressing

1 pkg. (1 oz.) HIDDEN VALLEY® ORIGINAL
    RANCH DRESSING MIX
1/4 cup WATER
1/4 cup VEGETABLE OIL
2 Tbsp. CIDER VINEGAR
1 Tbsp. LIGHT BROWN SUGAR
2 Tbsp. crumbled, cooked BACON

Whisk all ingredients together. Chill.

Dodge City

Called "Hell on the Plains" and the "Wickedest Little City in America," Dodge City was a wide-open town during the late 1800s. It is said that there was one well-stocked saloon there for every 20 citizens! Today, Dodge City is a major cattle-shipping point and serves as a supply and trade center for a large wheat-growing region. The Old West is revived here during Dodge City Days, the last weekend in July.

Hearty Bulgur Salad

A colorful, tasty way to add more fiber to the diet.

Kansas Wheat Commission—Manhattan

1 cup DRY BULGUR
2 cups warm WATER
2 cups peeled and diced
    CUCUMBER
1/2 cup thinly sliced GREEN
    ONIONS
1/2 cup diced GREEN BELL
    PEPPER

1 1/2 cups diced TOMATOES
10 RADISHES, diced
1/4 cup minced PARSLEY
1 tsp. SEASONED SALT
1/4 tsp. PEPPER
1/3 cup LEMON JUICE
1 Tbsp. minced MINT

Combine bulgur and water; let stand until bulgur is soft, about 20 minutes. Strain off excess liquid. In a large salad bowl, toss together all ingredients. Refrigerate until ready to serve.

Makes 6 cups.

Variation: Black olives, drained kidney beans and corn may be added.

About Bulgur

Bulgur is made by soaking and cooking the whole wheat kernel, drying it, then removing 5 percent of the bran and cracking the remaining kernel into small pieces.

Corn & Black Bean Salad

Karen Anderson—Wichita

1 cup cooked BLACK BEANS
1 cup frozen CORN
1 GREEN BELL PEPPER, chopped
1 ONION, chopped

1/2 cup chopped CELERY
RICE VINEGAR to taste
CUMIN to taste

Combine all vegetables in a glass serving bowl, add vinegar and cumin. Chill well.

Serves 4.

Main Dishes

Kansas Beef Stroganoff

"Kansas is noted for its great beef; this is one of the best beef recipes I have found."

Polly R. Bales—Logan

1 lb. BEEF SIRLOIN	1 clove GARLIC, minced
4 Tbsp. FLOUR	1 Tbsp. TOMATO PASTE
1/2 tsp. SALT	1 can (10.5 oz.) BEEF CONSOMMÉ
4 Tbsp. BUTTER	or 1 1/4 cups BEEF STOCK
1 cup thinly sliced fresh	1 cup SOUR CREAM
MUSHROOMS	2 Tbsp. SHERRY
1/2 cup chopped ONION	

On a cutting board, cut beef into 1/4-inch wide strips. Combine 2 tablespoons of flour with the salt; dredge beef strips in mixture. In a roasting pan, melt 2 tablespoons of butter; add beef and quickly brown on all sides. Add mushrooms, onion and garlic; cook 3-4 minutes or until onion is barely tender. Remove meat and mushrooms to a dish and set aside. Add the last 2 tablespoons of butter to pan drippings; when melted, blend in remaining flour. Add tomato paste and stir. Slowly add consommé, cooking on medium heat and stirring constantly until mixture thickens. Return beef and mushrooms to pan. Stir in sour cream and sherry; heat briefly. Serve with rice or noodles.

Serves 6-8.

Spicy Beef Roll-Ups

"My husband and I have our own ranch and therefore, our own meat. Sometimes we have too much beef so I've learned to cook creatively."

Charlene M. Wagner—Easton

1 1/2 lbs. ROUND STEAK,
   thinly sliced
1 cup cooked WHITE RICE
1/4 cup RAISINS
2 Tbsp. SHORTENING
1 can (10.5 oz.) ONION SOUP
1/2 soup can WATER

1/4 cup VINEGAR
1 Tbsp. BROWN SUGAR
6 WHOLE CLOVES
1 BAY LEAF
4 GINGERSNAPS, crumbled

On a cutting board, cut steak into six (8 x 4-inch) pieces; tenderize with a meat hammer. Combine rice and raisins; place a portion of mixture near center of each piece of steak; roll up, tucking in ends. Fasten with skewers or toothpicks. In a skillet, melt shortening; add steak rolls and brown and drain. Add remaining ingredients, except gingersnaps. Cover and simmer 1 1/4 hours or until tender. Remove cloves and bay leaf. Add gingersnaps and simmer for 15 minutes, stirring occasionally.

Serves 6.

Baked Fish in Sour Cream

"This is an old recipe and a family favorite."

Debby Greenstein—Business Dynamics, Inc., Overland Park

2 lbs. FISH FILLETS
2-3 Tbsp. BUTTER, melted
SALT and PEPPER to taste
1 cup SOUR CREAM with CHIVES

2 Tbsp. FLOUR
2 Tbsp. LEMON JUICE
1 cup grated CHEDDAR
   CHEESE

Layer fillets in a 9 x 13 baking dish. Brush with butter and season. In a bowl, combine sour cream, flour and lemon juice. Spoon over fillets; sprinkle with cheese. Bake, uncovered, at 375° for 25-30 minutes.

Serves 4-6.

The Baron's
Barbeque Chicken

This recipe from Paul Kirk (The Baron of Barbecue) was originally published in "The Passion of Barbeque."

Paul Kirk—Roeland Park

2 Tbsp. GARLIC SALT
1 Tbsp. PAPRIKA
1 Tbsp. BLACK PEPPER
2 FRYING CHICKENS, cut in half

Basting Sauce:
   1 cup WATER
   1 cup KETCHUP
   1/4 cup CIDER VINEGAR
   2 Tbsp. ONION FLAKES

   3 Tbsp. WORCESTERSHIRE
     SAUCE
   1 tsp. DRY MUSTARD

Mix garlic salt, paprika and pepper. Sprinkle over chicken, covering the entire surface. Place chicken on the grill skin-side-up over a medium-hot fire. Cover and grill for 30 minutes; turn and cook another 15 minutes. Make basting sauce by stirring the ingredients together in a small saucepan. Bring mixture to a boil, then turn down heat and simmer for 10 minutes. When chicken is tender, baste entire surface and cook for another 5 minutes; turn and baste again. Chicken is done when it is well-glazed (be careful not to burn).

Serves 4-6.

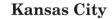

Kansas City

Often called the "Gateway to Kansas," this city lies on the Kansas-Missouri border, along both banks of the Kansas River. Kansas City is the chief industrial center of eastern Kansas with food processing ranking as the leading industry. Other products include automobiles, fiberglass and soap. It is also an agricultural center of the plains region of the U.S.

Prize-Winning Barbecued Ribs

This recipe is from Judith Fertig who was nominated in 1999 for two awards: one was by the International Association of Culinary Professionals and the other was the James Beard award. Both nominations were for her book "Prairie Home Cooking."

Judith Fertig—Overland Park

2 SLABS BABY BACK PORK RIBS (about 4 lbs., see note)
1 qt. APPLE JUICE

3-4 chunks HICKORY or APPLE WOOD for a smoker, or
APPLE WOOD CHIPS for a covered grill (soak in water for
30 minutes)
Spice rub:

2 Tbsp. BROWN SUGAR	1 Tbsp. freshly ground
1 Tbsp. GARLIC SALT	PEPPER
1 Tbsp. PAPRIKA	1 Tbsp. CELERY SEEDS

12 oz. BEER
2 cups TOMATO-BASED BARBECUE SAUCE

The night before cooking ribs, cover them with apple juice and refrigerate. The next day, build a fire in a smoker, or an indirect fire in a covered grill, to a temperature of 225° to 250°. Place a water pan next to the coals, or on the bottom rack of an electric smoker. When cooking temperature has been reached, add the wood. Remove the ribs from the marinade and pat them dry. In a small bowl, combine the spice rub ingredients. Rub spices onto the surface of the meat. Cook for 1 1/2 hours. Turn ribs over, baste them with the beer and cook for 1/2 hour more, basting every 10 minutes. Baste ribs with about 1 cup of the barbecue sauce, wrap in aluminum foil and smoke for 30 minutes more. Serve hot, with the remaining cup of sauce.

Note: One of the secrets to great ribs is to remove the bluish-white membrane on the back of each rib. Start at the narrow end and, using a paring knife, separate the membrane from the meat a little. Use needlenose pliers to pull off the rest of the membrane. (This process is easier if ribs are cold.)

Barbecued Rib Roast

*This recipe is from Paul Kirk (The Baron of Barbecue) and was
originally published in "Wild About Kansas City Barbecue."*

Paul Kirk—Roeland Park

1 (7 lb.) BONELESS RIB ROAST
LEMON PEPPER

Marinade:
1/2 cup WATER	4 stalks CELERY, diced
1 1/2 cups BURGUNDY WINE	2 cloves GARLIC, crushed
1/2 cup RED WINE VINEGAR	2 BAY LEAVES, crushed
1 med. ONION, thinly sliced	

Combine marinade ingredients and simmer for 20 minutes.
Remove from heat. Rub roast generously with lemon pepper,
then place meat and marinade mixture in a large resealable
plastic bag. Marinate in the refrigerator for 4 hours. Prepare
fire on one side of the grill. Remove roast from bag and place at
opposite end of grill from the fire. Cover and cook at 150° for 2
1/2 hours or 25 minutes per pound. Add moistened hickory
chunks to the fire periodically.

Serves 14-20.

Guy's Fuzzy Navel Steak

*This recipe is from Guy Simpson (The K.C. Rib Doctor) and
was originally published in "The Passion of Barbeque."*

Guy Simpson—Shawnee

1 (1-inch thick) SIRLOIN STEAK

Marinade:
3/4 cup ORANGE JUICE	1 Tbsp. K.C. RIB DOCTOR®
1/4 cup LIGHT SOY SAUCE	SEASONING (or other
1 clove GARLIC, minced	barbecue seasoning)
1/4 tsp. ground CLOVES	

Combine ingredients to make marinade. Place steak and
marinade in a sealable plastic bag and keep in refrigerator 2-4
hours, turning often. Drain off marinade and grill steak to
desired doneness (16 minutes for medium), turning once.

Rouladen

(German rolled steak)

"When my husband was an Army officer, we lived in Germany for seven years. This is a dish I learned to make while we were there."

Teresa J. Hicks—Lansing

12 slices BACON
SALT and PEPPER to taste
6 strips TOP ROUND BEEF,
   thinly sliced
GREY POUPON® MUSTARD
6 WHOLE DILL PICKLES
1 sm. ONION, sliced
1 can (4.5 oz.) MUSHROOMS, undrained

3 Tbsp. instant BEEF
   BOUILLON
1/4 cup KETCHUP
2-2 1/2 cups WATER
1 Tbsp. CORNSTARCH
EVAPORATED MILK
Cooked NOODLES

In a skillet, fry bacon slices and reserve drippings. Salt and pepper one side of beef strips; spread with mustard. Lay 2 bacon slices on top of each strip. Place a pickle on top of the bacon, roll strips up, securing with a toothpick. In a deep pan, add bacon drippings, beef rolls and onion; brown. Combine mushrooms, beef bouillon, ketchup and water; pour over meat. Add enough water to cover beef with liquids. Cook on low heat for 3-4 hours or place in crockpot and cook on low for 6-8 hours. When ready to serve, remove beef rolls from sauce. Combine cornstarch with a small amount of milk and add to sauce to thicken. Heat thoroughly. Place beef rolls on top of cooked noodles and spoon sauce over all.

Serves 4-6.

Did You Know?

The Geodetic Center of North America is about 40 miles south of Lebanon, Kansas, at Meade's Ranch. When a surveyor checks a property line anywhere in North America, that surveyor is checking the position of property in relation to Meade's Ranch!

Super Pork Chops

Marva Lee Doud—Salina

4-6 (1/2-inch thick) PORK CHOPS
1/4 cup chopped ONION
2 CARROTS, grated
1 can (15 oz.) WHITE POTATOES, drained and sliced
2 Tbsp. BROWN SUGAR
1 can (14 oz.) BAVARIAN-STYLE SAUERKRAUT
1 can (10.75 oz.) CREAM OF CELERY SOUP

In a skillet, brown pork chops; set aside. In a 9 x 13 baking dish, mix onion, carrots, potatoes and brown sugar. Top mixture with the sauerkraut. Arrange pork chops on top of the sauerkraut; spread soup over the chops. Bake at 350° for 45-60 minutes or until pork chops are thoroughly cooked.

Serves 4.

Cowboy Beans with Beef

"This is a great dish for picnics."

Leon "Butch" Cuppet—Savonburg

1 Tbsp. MARGARINE
2 lbs. GROUND BEEF
1 can (15.5 oz.) GREAT NORTHERN BEANS
1 can (16 oz.) BUTTER BEANS
1 can (15 oz.) KIDNEY BEANS
1 can (16 oz.) PORK & BEANS
1 GREEN BELL PEPPER, chopped
1 med. ONION, chopped
1 cup BARBECUE SAUCE

In a skillet, melt margarine; add beef and brown then drain. In a crockpot, add beans, bell pepper and onion. Place beef on top of mixture. Pour barbecue sauce on top of the beef. DO NOT STIR. Cook on low heat for 2 hours, then on high heat for 1 hour.

Serves 8-10.

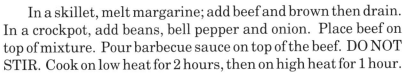

Vegetable Pie

*"This is such a wonderful recipe for using all the
fresh garden vegetables."*

Kathy Hogue—Mission Valley Ranch, Topeka

2 Tbsp. VEGETABLE OIL
2 cloves GARLIC, chopped
3 med. TOMATOES, chopped
2 sm. ONIONS, chopped
1 sm. EGGPLANT, peeled, quartered and sliced
1 sm. GREEN BELL PEPPER, sliced
1 cup CORN
SALT and PEPPER to taste
3 med. ZUCCHINI, sliced
6 Tbsp. grated PARMESAN CHEESE
1 (9-inch) unbaked PIE SHELL
2 Tbsp. BUTTER, cut into pieces

Preheat oven to 350°. In a large skillet, heat oil and garlic
over medium heat. Add tomatoes, onion, eggplant, bell pepper,
corn, salt and pepper. Sauté until vegetables are crisp-tender.
Stir in zucchini and continue to cook until zucchini is crisp-
tender. Sprinkle 2 tablespoons of cheese over the bottom of the
pie shell. Using a slotted spoon, add one-half of the vegetables.
Sprinkle with another 2 tablespoons of cheese; dot with 1
tablespoon of butter. Add remaining vegetables and sprinkle
with last 2 tablespoons of cheese; dot with remaining butter.
Bake for 40 minutes or until crust is golden brown. Serve hot.

Serves 6-8.

Movies in Kansas

The movies Mars Attacks!, Picnic, Paper
Moon, The Day After, Sarah Plain and Tall,
Mr. & Mrs. Bridge, Kansas, Nice Girls Don't
Explode, Where Pigeons Go to Die, Cross of
Fire, In Cold Blood *and* Truman *were all
filmed in Kansas.*

Chicken à la King

"I lived on a farm near a creek in Leavenworth County during the war. We had chickens available or we could just fish in the creek nearby. This became a favorite with our family because we could make it with either chicken or baked fish."

Alberta C. Welch—Rapid City

4 Tbsp. BUTTER
4 Tbsp. finely chopped GREEN BELL PEPPER
1 Tbsp. FLOUR
1 tsp. SALT
2 cups MILK
2 cups diced, cooked CHICKEN
2 Tbsp. chopped PIMENTOS
1/2 cup chopped MUSHROOMS
4 slices TOAST or baked PASTRY SHELLS

In a large skillet, melt butter, add bell pepper and sauté until soft. Mix flour with salt and add to skillet and stir until well-blended. Pour in milk, stirring until smooth. Add chicken, pimentos and mushrooms; mix. Serve on warm toast or in pastry shells.

Serves 4.

Mom's Chicken Casserole

"This is a family favorite."

Esther Clapham—Larned

3 1/2 cups diced, cooked CHICKEN
1 pkg. (12 oz.) NOODLES, cooked
2 Tbsp. chopped ONION
3 1/2 cups CHICKEN BROTH
1 1/2 cups lightly crushed CORNFLAKES

In a bowl, mix together all ingredients, except cornflakes. Pour into a 9 x 13 baking pan. Sprinkle the cornflakes over the top. Bake at 350° for 45-55 minutes or until brown on top. May be prepared ahead of time and refrigerated.

Serves 12.

Stroganoff-Style Meatballs

"This recipe is a quick dish, perfect for a busy family or for a neighborhood potluck. I won 2nd Place with this dish in the Lyon County Cook-Off almost 30 years ago."

Belle Grimsley—Americus

1 1/2 lbs. GROUND CHUCK
1 EGG
SALT and PEPPER to taste
1/4 cup fine dry BREAD
    CRUMBS
1/3 cup MILK
1 tsp. grated LEMON PEEL
3 Tbsp. minced ONION
1 Tbsp. BUTTER

1 can (4.5 oz.) sliced
    MUSHROOMS, drained
2 Tbsp. FLOUR
1 tsp. STEAK SAUCE
1 can (10.75 oz.) BEEF
    CONSOMMÉ
1 Tbsp. dried PARSLEY
1/2 cup SOUR CREAM
Cooked NOODLES

In a mixing bowl, lightly mix the first seven ingredients and 1 tablespoon of the onion. Shape into 18 meatballs. In a skillet, melt butter and add meatballs; brown on all sides. Remove meatballs and set aside. Lightly brown mushrooms in the drippings in the skillet. Add remaining onion and blend in flour and steak sauce. Stir in remaining ingredients, except sour cream, and bring to a boil. Add meatballs, cover and simmer for 15 minutes. Remove meatballs to a hot serving dish. Stir sour cream into the sauce in the skillet, season to taste and pour over meatballs. Serve over warm noodles.

Serves 4-6.

Amelia Earhart

Born in Atchison, Kansas, Amelia Earhart became the first woman to cross the Atlantic Ocean by air and the first woman to fly it alone. She was also the first woman to receive the Distinguished Flying Cross. Her plane vanished near Howland Island in the Pacific Ocean in 1937 as she tried to fly around the world.

Smothered Round Steak

"When my father was in the Scouts, his troop would make this recipe over the campfire."

Anita Phillips—Great Bend

4 lbs. ROUND STEAK	3 cans (10.75 oz. ea.) CREAM
FLOUR	OF MUSHROOM SOUP
1 Tbsp. VEGETABLE OIL	1 1/2 soup cans of WATER

Cut steak into desired number of servings. Dredge pieces in flour to coat well. In a skillet or Dutch oven, heat oil; add steak and slowly brown on both sides. Drain; add soup and water. Simmer slowly until the meat is tender. If sauce thickens too much, add a small amount of water while cooking. Serve with mashed potatoes or noodles.

Serves 12-16.

Green Pepper Steak

"This recipe was thrown together from scratch. Our family loves it!"

Mary Carson—Quenemo

1 or 2 lbs. ROUND or CHUCK STEAK
1 Tbsp. BUTTER
1 can (4.5 oz.) MUSHROOMS, with juice
1 lg. ONION, diced
1 lg. GREEN BELL PEPPER, chopped
2 cans (10.75 oz. ea.) BEEF BROTH
2 tsp. KITCHEN BOUQUET®
1 Tbsp. CORNSTARCH
1/4-1/2 cup WATER

Slice steak into 1/4-inch thick strips or chunks. In a skillet, melt butter and brown meat. Add mushrooms, onion, bell pepper, broth and Kitchen Bouquet; simmer 1 3/4 hours or until meat is tender. Mix cornstarch with water to make a thickening paste; add to skillet and continue to simmer until desired consistency. Serve with rice or mashed potatoes.

Serves 4-8.

Hearty Harvest Casserole

"This is an old recipe that my mother always used. We live in southwest Kansas where we often need something fast and nutritious for harvest time meals in the summer. It is fairly fast to put together and does not need much to go with it."

Pat Habiger—Spearville

1 lb. GROUND BEEF
1 lb. BULK PORK SAUSAGE
1 lg. ONION, chopped
1 1/2 cups uncooked LONG GRAIN RICE
1 can (10.75 oz.) CREAM OF MUSHROOM SOUP
1 can (10.75 oz.) CREAMY ONION SOUP
1 can (10.75 oz.) CREAM OF CHICKEN SOUP
1 lg. GREEN BELL PEPPER, chopped
2 stalks CELERY, chopped

In a skillet, sauté beef and sausage with onion until brown; drain. Add remaining ingredients, mix well and place in a greased 4-quart baking dish. Cover tightly and bake at 350° for 40-50 minutes.

Serves 12-16.

Baked Beans Kansas-Style

"This is an original recipe that I have created by trying different ways to 'spice-up' traditional baked beans."

Letty Wasserman—Overland Park

1 lb. GROUND CHUCK
1 med. ONION, diced
1 cup BARBECUE SAUCE
1/4 cup MUSTARD
2 cans (16 oz. ea.) VEGETARIAN BAKED BEANS
1/4 cup packed BROWN SUGAR
1 cup grated CHEDDAR CHEESE

In a skillet, brown beef with onion; drain. Add sauce, mustard, beans and brown sugar; simmer for 15 minutes. Pour into a serving dish and top with cheese.

Serves 6-8.

Southwestern-Style Quiche

"We raise wheat on our farm and we also have chickens so we always have fresh eggs. I add sliced fresh tomatoes or chives from our garden to the top of this dish to give it a colorful look."

Mary Reese—Creek Side Farm, Fowler

1 (10-inch) lightly baked PIE SHELL
3/4 cup shredded CHEDDAR CHEESE
1 can (4 oz.) diced GREEN CHILES, drained
8 EGGS, slightly beaten
1/2 cup SKIM MILK
1/2 tsp. CHILI POWDER
1/2 tsp. ONION POWDER
SALT and PEPPER to taste
1/2 cup PICANTE SAUCE
TOMATO SLICES
CHIVES, chopped

Sprinkle cheese in bottom of pie shell and add chiles. In a bowl, combine eggs with milk, chili powder, onion powder, salt and pepper. Pour over cheese mixture and dot with picante sauce. Wrap aluminum foil around edges of pie to protect crust from burning, then bake at 350° for 25-30 minutes or until knife inserted in the center comes out clean. Cut into wedges. Garnish with tomato slices and chives.

Serves 6-8.

Kansas Buffalo

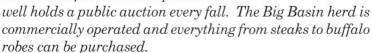

The three largest herds of buffalo (bison) in Kansas are located on public lands at the Maxwell Game Preserve (McPherson), Big Basin (Ashland) and Buffalo Game Preserve (Garden City). More than 200 head can be found on each preserve. Maxwell holds a public auction every fall. The Big Basin herd is commercially operated and everything from steaks to buffalo robes can be purchased.

Cimarron Flank Steak

"I received this recipe from my friend, Karen Gould, who is one of the greatest Kansas cooks I know."

Kathleen Holt—Cimarron Hotel & Restaurant (est. 1886), Cimarron

Marinade:
  1/4 cup SOY SAUCE
  3 Tbsp. HONEY
  2 Tbsp. VINEGAR
  1 1/2 tsp. GINGER
  1 1/2 tsp. GARLIC POWDER
  1 GREEN ONION, chopped
  3/4 cup SALAD OIL
1 1/2 lbs. FLANK STEAK

In a large bowl, combine all marinade ingredients and stir well. Add meat and marinate overnight. Broil or grill steaks for 2-3 minutes on each side for medium rare to medium doneness. Slice across the grain into thin slices.

Serves 4.

Pheasant Casserole

"This recipe is easy to prepare."

Marion Bogart—Kensington

SALT
PHEASANT, cut up
FLOUR
1 stick BUTTER, sliced

1 med. ONION, thinly sliced
SALT and PEPPER to taste
1/2 cup WATER

Salt each piece of pheasant then flour lightly. Place 1/2 of the slices of butter on the bottom of a deep casserole dish. Cover with onion slices. Place pheasant in casserole and add salt and pepper. Cover with remaining slices of butter and add water. Roast at 250°, covered, for 4-5 hours. A delicious gravy forms while roasting which can be served over rice or potatoes.

Caribbean Chicken Breasts

National winner of the annual Chicken Council contest.

National Chicken Council—Mary King, Ulysses

4 boneless, skinless CHICKEN
    BREAST HALVES
1/2 tsp. ground CORIANDER
1/4 tsp. ground GINGER
1/2 tsp. ground CUMIN
1/8 tsp. CAYENNE PEPPER
1 Tbsp. VEGETABLE OIL

1/4 cup fresh LEMON JUICE
3 Tbsp. fresh ORANGE JUICE
3 Tbsp. fresh LIME JUICE
1/3 cup MANGO CHUTNEY
    with JALAPEÑOS
CILANTRO SPRIGS
RED CHILE PEPPERS

In a small dish, mix together the coriander, ginger, cumin and cayenne. Rub mixture over chicken breasts. In a skillet, heat oil. Add chicken and cook until fork can be inserted with ease. Remove to platter and keep warm. Add juices and chutney to skillet; bring to a boil. Cook, stirring until mixture begins to thicken. Pour over chicken. Garnish with cilantro sprigs and red chile peppers.

Serves 4.

Brett's Beans

"A young man named Brett gave me this recipe. I serve these beans at every pig roast. The recipe may be doubled or tripled."

Martha Sue Olander—Linwood

1 lb. BACON
1 med. ONION, chopped
CHILI POWDER to taste
2 lbs. GROUND BEEF
2 cups BARBECUE SAUCE
1 cup packed BROWN SUGAR

1 cup SUGAR
1 cup lg. LIMA BEANS
1 cup lg. BUTTER BEANS
1 lg. can (21 oz.) PORK and
    BEANS
1 cup RED KIDNEY BEANS

In a skillet, fry bacon slices until crisp then drain and set aside. Mix onion and chili powder with the beef; brown. In a large baking dish, combine barbecue sauce and sugars; mix well. Drain beans and add to mixture. Stir in bacon and ground beef. Bake at 350° for 1-1 1/2 hours.

Serves 8-10.

Pepperloin Steak with Mustard Sauce

"In the late 1800s, the Kansas City area was a thriving stockyard center. This beef recipe was created in the kitchen of one of the hotels of that era."

Nancy Darish—Overland Park

4 lbs. BEEF TENDERLOIN
KOSHER SALT
Coarsely ground PEPPER
2 med. ONIONS, sliced
1 BAY LEAF
1 clove GARLIC, crushed
1/2 cup VEGETABLE OIL

Combine salt and pepper; coat entire tenderloin by rubbing on mixture. Place in a glass baking dish with sliced onions, bay leaf and garlic; cover with oil. Marinate in refrigerator for 2-3 days turning beef 1 or 2 times. Drain beef and sear on charcoal grill. Cook approximately 25 minutes; slice into medallions. Serve with **Mustard Sauce.**

Serves 8-10.

Mustard Sauce

1 Tbsp. BUTTER
3 Tbsp. chopped ONION
2 GREEN ONIONS, chopped
1/2 clove GARLIC, crushed
2 oz. WHITE WINE
1 BAY LEAF
1 WHOLE CLOVE
10-12 sprigs fresh PARSLEY

1 Tbsp. BROWN SUGAR
1 cup CIDER VINEGAR
3 Tbsp. DRY MUSTARD
1/2 cup MUSTARD
Pinch of THYME
Pinch of OREGANO
4 cups BROWN GRAVY
Dash of TABASCO®

In a skillet, melt butter then add onions and sauté until translucent. Add garlic, wine, bay leaf, clove, parsley, brown sugar, vinegar, and mustards. Mix well and then add thyme and oregano. Stir in gravy and cook slowly for 30 minutes. Strain sauce and stir in Tabasco. Continue cooking over low heat for 25 minutes.

Chicken Victoria

Diane Balanoff—Leawood

2 Tbsp. FLOUR
SALT and PEPPER to taste
GARLIC SALT to taste
PAPRIKA to taste
1 WHOLE FRYING CHICKEN, cut up
3 Tbsp. OIL
1/4 cup slivered ALMONDS
1 sm. ONION, chopped
1 cup chopped CELERY
1 can (4.5 oz.) sliced MUSHROOMS
Fresh PARSLEY, chopped
3/4 cup DRY SACK SHERRY (do not substitute)

In a bowl, combine flour, salt, pepper, garlic salt and paprika. Dredge chicken pieces in flour mixture to coat. In a skillet, heat 2 tablespoons of oil, add almonds and brown. Remove almonds and set aside. Place chicken in the skillet, brown on all sides and then transfer to a baking dish. Heat 1 tablespoon of oil and sauté onions, celery, mushrooms and parsley for 3 minutes. Add sherry; bring to a boil. Remove from heat and add almonds. Pour mixture over chicken. Refrigerate until ready to bake. Bake at 325° for 1 1/2-2 hours.

Serves 4.

Broiled Quail

"This is a family favorite."

Marion Bogart—Kennsington

4 - 6 QUAIL BREASTS
WHITE WINE (optional)
1 pkg. (12 oz.) BACON
1/3 cup BUTTER, melted

If desired, marinate quail in wine for 4-12 hours. Wrap each quail breast with bacon and secure with toothpicks. Broil in oven or outside on grill, basting with butter.

Mostaccioli Primavera

National Sunflower Association

12 oz. (3 cups) uncooked MOSTACCIOLI
4 Tbsp. SUNFLOWER OIL
1 RED PEPPER, julienned
2 CARROTS, julienned
2 small ZUCCHINI, julienned
2/3 cup fresh ORIENTAL PEA PODS cut in halves
3 GREEN ONIONS, sliced
1 1/2 cups diced TOMATOES
2 Tbsp. chopped CHIVES
2 Tbsp. fresh DILL (or 1/2 tsp. dried DILL)
SALT and PEPPER to taste
1/4 cup toasted SUNFLOWER KERNELS

Cook mostaccioli in lightly salted water until al dente (don't overcook). Heat sunflower oil in a large nonstick skillet. Add red pepper and carrots and sauté for approximately 6 minutes. Add zucchini, pea pods and onions and steam for five minutes. Add the tomatoes, chopped chives and finely chopped dill. Season with salt and pepper and heat until warmed through. Toss the vegetable mixture with the drained mostaccioli. Sprinkle with toasted sunflower kernels.

Potato Burritos

Lucinda Anstaett—Newton

2 lbs. LEAN GROUND BEEF
1 lg. ONION, finely diced
1 stick MARGARINE
1/2 cup WATER
3 cans (4 oz. ea.) diced GREEN CHILES

SALT and PEPPER to taste
2 lb. bag frozen HASH BROWN POTATOES
FLOUR TORTILLAS
Grated CHEDDAR CHEESE
PICANTE SAUCE

Place beef and onion in a skillet and brown. Add margarine, water, green chiles, salt, pepper and hash browns. Cover and steam for 20 minutes. Mash with potato masher. Place a generous portion of mixture on tortillas, roll up tightly and reheat. When ready to serve, sprinkle with grated cheese. Serve with picante sauce on the side.

Side Dishes

Kyselé Zeli
(Cabbage with Caraway)

"This is a Czechoslovakian recipe, the 'soul food' on which I was raised. One can find it served at get-togethers all along the Kansas-Oklahoma border where many third generation Czech-Americans reside."

Anna K. Petrik—Wind, Earth and Sky, Caldwell

1 cup WATER
1 med. CABBAGE, chopped
1 ONION, minced
1 tsp. SUGAR
1 Tbsp. SHORTENING

1/2 sm. ONION, chopped
1 Tbsp. FLOUR
2 Tbsp. WATER
1 or 2 Tbsp. CARAWAY
    SEEDS

In a covered kettle, simmer water, cabbage, minced onion and sugar for 30 minutes or until cabbage is tender; drain off half of the water. In a Dutch oven, combine the shortening and chopped onion, sauté until translucent and add cabbage mixture. Blend flour and water to make a smooth paste and add to mixture. Stir in caraway seeds. Slowly bring to a boil, stirring gently, and cook until seeds are softened. Serve hot or cold.

Serves 4.

Aunt Mary's Ketchup

Bunny Adams—Atwood

1 Tbsp. ALLSPICE
1 Tbsp. MUSTARD SEEDS
5 qts. TOMATOES
1 1/2 cups SUGAR
2 cups VINEGAR

2 tsp. CINNAMON
1 tsp. PAPRIKA
3 Tbsp. SALT
1 tsp. PEPPER

Place allspice and mustard seeds on a small piece of cheese-cloth and tie into a "spice bag." In a pot, cover tomatoes with water and add spice bag. Simmer on medium heat until the tomatoes are softened, then press them through a sieve, reserving the juice. Add remaining ingredients to juice and cook slowly until thickened.

Yields 7 pints.

Did You Know?
At one time it was against the law to serve ice cream on cherry pie in Kansas.

Corn Pudding

"I have found this to be a tasty way to serve corn."

Frances Wienck—Barnes

1 can (15.25 oz) WHOLE KERNEL CORN, drained
1 can (14.75 oz.) CREAM-STYLE CORN
1 cup MILK
2 EGGS, beaten
1/4 cup MARGARINE or BUTTER, melted
1/4 tsp. PEPPER
1/2 cup CORNMEAL

In a large bowl, combine both cans of corn, milk, eggs, margarine and pepper. Add cornmeal and stir until it is moistened. Pour the mixture into a 2-quart casserole dish. Bake at 350° for 50-60 minutes or until set and lightly browned.

Serves 8.

Black Bean, Corn & Mushroom Relish

Wendy Clasten—Leawood

1 ONION, chopped
1 Tbsp. BUTTER
1 can (15 oz.) BLACK BEANS, drained
1 can (8 oz.) MUSHROOMS, undrained
2 cans (15.25 oz. ea.) CORN, drained
1/4 cup SOY SAUCE
1 Tbsp. CUMIN or to taste
1 tsp. GARLIC POWDER
PEPPER to taste

In a saucepan, sauté onion in butter until translucent. Add beans, mushrooms and corn. Stir and simmer for 15 minutes. Add soy sauce, cumin, garlic powder and pepper. Stir and simmer for 5 minutes.

Yields 6-7 cups.

Schmier Käse

(Cooked Cottage Cheese)

"This is a German dish that my Great-grandma Sauer and my Grandma Riedel always made."

Cindy Flax—Hays

2 cups DRY COTTAGE CHEESE   1/2 tsp. SALT
2 EGGS, beaten   2 tsp. SHORTENING
1 tsp. BAKING SODA

In a bowl, combine cottage cheese, eggs, baking soda and salt. Heat skillet and melt shortening. Pour cheese mixture into skillet and cook over low heat until the cheese is melted; stir until well-blended and smooth. Pour onto a buttered platter and cool. Slice thin to serve. If desired, use hot as a spread.

Yam & Apple Casserole

"I adapted this recipe from a cooking show on TV and make it as a special Thanksgiving and Christmas dish. It is delicious!"

Mildred P. Kinder—Leavenworth

2 cans (15 oz. ea.) YAMS, drained and sliced
1 or 2 TART APPLES, thinly sliced
1/2 cup packed LIGHT BROWN SUGAR
2 Tbsp. SHERRY (optional)
1 tsp. CINNAMON
4 Tbsp. MARGARINE

In a casserole dish, arrange layers of yams and apples, ending with apples on top. Sprinkle each layer with brown sugar, cinnamon and sherry. Dot top layer with margarine. Cover casserole dish and bake at 350° for 30 minutes or until apples are very tender.

Serves 6.

Orange Noodle Casserole

"This recipe has been handed down from generation to generation. It is a Jewish 'kugel' or noodle casserole."

Debby Greenstein—Business Dynamics, Inc., Overland Park

1 stick BUTTER, softened
1/2 cup SUGAR
3 EGGS, separated
12 oz. SOUR CREAM
12 oz. COTTAGE CHEESE
1 tsp. VANILLA
1/2 cup ORANGE JUICE
PEEL of 1 ORANGE, grated
8 oz. WIDE NOODLES, cooked

In a bowl, cream butter and sugar together; beat in egg yolks one at a time. Add sour cream, cottage cheese, vanilla, orange juice and grated orange peel. Fold in noodles. In another bowl, beat egg whites until stiff and fold into noodle mixture. Place mixture in a 9 x 13 baking dish; bake at 350° for 1 hour.

Serves 10-12.

Mom's Chili Sauce

"I won the Blue Ribbon at the 1999 Leavenworth County Fair with this recipe. This is one of my children's favorites."

Jacki Cahill—Lansing

1 peck (16 lbs.) TOMATOES
2 lbs. ONIONS
1 RED BELL PEPPER
3 GREEN BELL PEPPERS
2 HOT BANANA PEPPERS
1 stalk CELERY
1 Tbsp. WHOLE CLOVES
2 sticks CINNAMON, broken

1 Tbsp. WHOLE MUSTARD
SEEDS
1 Tbsp. WHOLE ALLSPICE
1/4 cup SALT
1 qt. CIDER VINEGAR
2 cups SUGAR
2 cups packed BROWN
SUGAR

In a large pot of boiling water, scald tomatoes. Peel and chop tomatoes, return to pot and simmer on medium heat for 15 minutes; drain off 1/2 of the liquid. Chop onions, peppers and celery and add to pot. Simmer for 1 1/2 hours. Place spices on a small piece of cheese cloth and tie into a "spice bag". Add spice bag, vinegar, and both sugars to simmering ingredients and continue to cook for 1 1/2 hours longer or to desired thickness. Remove spice bag. Pour into hot, sterilized jars to within 1/2 inch of top. Wash and scald jar lids. Place lid on each jar and screw cap on tightly. Place jars in a pan with enough water to come up to the rim of the jars. Bring to a boil and boil for 15 minutes. Remove jars, wipe clean and let cool. Lids will 'pop' as they seal.

Pony Express

On April 3, 1860, the freighting firm of Russell, Majors & Waddell, of Leavenworth, undertook the task of creating a pony express mail service. They set up 190 stations, with 400 keepers and assistants, 400 horses and 80 riders. The riders rode day and night in all kinds of weather. In a total of 650,000 miles, the mail was lost only once. The service ended on Oct. 24, 1861 due to the advent of the telegraph.

Fried Carrots

"I grew up during the depression. My parents had a large garden and grew many of our vegetables. I especially remember these fried carrots that my mother fixed for our meals."

Edna Ohlsen—Horton

6-8 lg. CARROTS	**1 cup FLOUR**
3/4 cup WATER	**1 tsp. SALT**
2 EGGS	**COOKING OIL**

In a skillet, cook carrots in 1/2 cup of water until softened. Drain water then slice carrots lengthwise into strips. In a bowl, lightly beat eggs and add flour, salt and remaining water to make a thin batter. Add a small amount of oil to skillet and heat. Dip carrot strips into the batter and fry until golden brown.

Serves 6-8.

Squash Casserole

"Home-grown squash is plentiful in Kansas during the summer months. This recipe offers a unique way to serve up a 'straight-forward' vegetable."

Marci Kellner—Kehilath Israel Montessori Preschool, Stilwell

6 med. YELLOW SQUASH, coarsely chopped
6 med. GREEN SQUASH, coarsely chopped
3 med. CARROTS, coarsely chopped
1 ONION, chopped
1 cup PEPPERIDGE FARM® DRESSING
1 EGG, beaten
2 Tbsp. BUTTER
SALT and PEPPER to taste

In a saucepan, boil squash, carrots and onion until tender. Drain water. Mash vegetables lightly. Add dressing, egg, butter, salt and pepper; mix well. Pour into a buttered casserole dish. Bake at 350° for 1 hour.

Serves 6-8.

Farm House Potatoes

"This was a favorite at Farm House Fraternity at Kansas State University during the 1920s. Our housemother, Faire French of Pretty Prairie, introduced this recipe to Farm House."

Gary Anderson—LandMark Inn at the Historic Bank of Oberlin, Oberlin

1 pkg. (32 oz.) frozen HASH BROWN POTATOES
1/2 cup chopped ONION
2 cups grated CHEDDAR CHEESE
1 can (10.75 oz.) CREAM OF MUSHROOM SOUP
2 cups SOUR CREAM
PEPPER to taste
1/2 cup crushed CORNFLAKES
1/4 cup BUTTER, melted

Mix first six ingredients in a large bowl. Spread on a greased cookie sheet or in a 9 x 13 baking pan. Mix cornflakes and butter. Spread over the potato mixture. Bake at 350° for 1 hour.

Serves 8-10.

Corn Fritters

"This is a delicious way to serve our abundant Kansas crop."

Susan Rosenthal—Leawood

1 1/2 cups FLOUR
2 tsp. BAKING POWDER
1/4 tsp. SALT
2 Tbsp. SUGAR
1 EGG, beaten

3/4 cup MILK
1 can (15.25 oz.) CORN, drained
COOKING OIL

Sift dry ingredients into a large bowl. In another bowl, combine egg and milk; gradually add to dry mixture. Stir in corn. Heat oil in a skillet and carefully drop corn batter by teaspoonfuls into hot oil. Fry 3-5 minutes or until golden brown. Sprinkle with powdered sugar if desired.

Serves 6.

The 101 Ranch

The matriarch of the 101, Ruth Miller, was not only the "chief cook and bottle washer," but ran this large spread in the sandhills of Edwards and Kiowa counties in Kansas. Her husband, Hugh Miller, founder, was the first to drive cattle from Mexico to Kansas. He died at an early age after establishing routes from the south and north to Kansas terminals for rail shipments east to Kansas City and Chicago. Ruth was left to raise two boys and two girls, operate a restaurant and oversee the ranch operations. Ruth lived to be 100 years old. Now, her son Jack Hugh Miller, sole survivor and 81 years old, is the current operator and historian. This is his remembrance of how this recipe came to be.

"While cooking the extra field corn that was bountiful that year, and experimenting with what to do with all the excess before spoilage set in, Mom was also the deciding vote in family arguments, boss and cowboy arguments as well as those which flared up after a few partakings of the finest bourbon of the time. What kept Mom safe was a high counter surrounding the cookstove. Not so unusual in ranch houses, but significant in this story because that is where someone's drink often was placed while they argued, with their hands doing most of the talking. This time it was Jack Hubert's drink. While flailing hands went everywhere, the critical move was the one which knocked his drink over. You guessed it, it poured right into the pot of boiling corn! The smell went so well with the corn that no one noticed and, fortunately, Mom had her back turned and did not notice either."

This story has several versions from being retold whenever this dish is served!

For Jack Miller—Miller's 101 Ranch, Kinsley

by Jerome J. Herrmann, MSW

PS: When Hugh Miller ended his first cattle drive from Northern Mexico to the U.S., his cowboys celebrated at a local saloon. He named his ranch for the amount of damages he paid for that celebration—$101.

The 101 Ranch Bourbon & Branch Water Corn Bake

For Jack Miller—Miller's 101 Ranch, Kinsley

3 lg. EGGS
1 1/4 cups EVAPORATED MILK
3 cups canned CREAM STYLE
    CORN
3 cups canned WHOLE KERNEL
    CORN, drained
3 Tbsp. BUTTER, melted

3 Tbsp. packed BROWN
    SUGAR
3 Tbsp. CORNSTARCH
3/4 tsp. NUTMEG
SALT and PEPPER to taste
4 1/2 Tbsp. BOURBON
3 Tbsp. PURIFIED WATER

Preheat oven to 350°. Generously butter a 2-qt. baking dish. Beat eggs and milk in a large bowl until thickened. Stir in corn, butter, brown sugar, cornstarch, nutmeg, salt and pepper. Pour into baking dish and bake for 45 minutes or until top browns and splits. Mix bourbon and water; pour on top and bake approximately 5-10 minutes longer or until a knife inserted in the middle comes out clean. Serve with a **KING CUT of KANSAS BEEF** broiled to your choice of doneness.

Trail Ride Version

*This is the 101 Ranch's method of keeping the **Corn Bake** from spoiling when a cattle drive becomes unpredictable.*

4 SERRANO CHILES, seeded and diced

Add chiles to recipe above. The chiles and bourbon will keep the cream and corn from becoming rancid.

Raisin-Prune Pudding

"This is a German dish known as 'Pluma Moos' that is served for Christmas and other special occasions. It is usually served with ham and fried potatoes. The recipe was brought from Russia by the Mennonites who settled near Goessel and Newton."

Geneva Pryce—Newton

2 cups RAISINS
1 cup PRUNES
3 pints WATER
3/4 cup SUGAR

1/2 cup FLOUR
1/2 tsp. SALT
3 cups MILK

In a medium pot, add the fruit and water and cook until almost soft. Add 1/2 cup of sugar during the last 5 minutes of cooking time. In a bowl, mix flour, 1/4 cup of sugar, salt and milk to make a thickening paste. Slowly add paste to the fruit mixture, stirring constantly until the mixture comes to a boil; allow to cool. Milk or water can be added to thin the mixture if necessary.

Serves 12.

Cherry Moos: Fresh or canned cherries can be used instead of the raisins and prunes to make this variation. Add an additional 1/2 cup of sugar in the first cooking stage of the recipe.

Rhubarb Conserve

"This recipe was given to me by my aunt. I feel extremely fortunate that she shared this recipe with me."

Belle Grimsley—Americus

3 ORANGES
3 lbs. RHUBARB
3 lbs. SUGAR

1/2 lb. shelled PECANS,
    scalded and chopped
1 lb. RAISINS, washed

Peel the oranges; chop the rinds in a food chopper; slice the pulp. Cut rhubarb into 1/2-inch pieces. Combine orange peels and slices and rhubarb in a saucepan. Add sugar, pecans and raisins. Cook over low heat for 45 minutes. Test as you would for jelly. Pour into glasses or canning jars and seal.

Mom's Dilly Bread

"This bread is always on our table for special occasion dinners such as Christmas, Thanksgiving and Easter."

Melissa A. Hicks—Lansing

1 pkg. ACTIVE DRY YEAST
1/4 cup warm WATER
1 cup COTTAGE CHEESE, heated to lukewarm
2 Tbsp. SUGAR
1 Tbsp. ONION FLAKES
2 tsp. DILL SEED
1 tsp. SALT
1 EGG, beaten
2 1/4 to 3 cups ALL-PURPOSE FLOUR
1 Tbsp. BUTTER or MARGARINE, softened
SALT

Dissolve yeast in warm water. In a mixing bowl, combine the next six ingredients. Add enough flour to make a dough that is easy to handle and not sticky. Let rise until doubled in bulk; punch down. Knead for a short time; let rise again until doubled in bulk. Place dough in a well-greased 8-inch round baking dish. Bake at 350° for 40-45 minutes. Brush with butter and sprinkle with salt while still warm.

Pumpkin-Date Bread

"Our neighbor grinds wheat into flour and gives it to us as a gift. It is very good in this recipe."

Merrill Powers—Spearville

1/3 cup MARGARINE, softened
3 Tbsp. BROWN SUGAR
EGG SUBSTITUTE equal to 2 eggs
1 cup canned PUMPKIN
1 cup WHOLE-WHEAT FLOUR
1 cup ALL-PURPOSE FLOUR
1 tsp. BAKING POWDER
1 tsp. BAKING SODA
1 1/2 tsp. CINNAMON
1/2 tsp. NUTMEG
1/4 tsp. ground CLOVES
1/4 tsp. ALLSPICE
1/4 tsp. SALT
1/2 cup BUTTERMILK
1 cup QUICK-COOKING OATS
1/2 cup chopped DATES

In a mixing bowl, cream margarine and brown sugar. Beat in egg substitute and pumpkin. In a separate bowl, combine the dry ingredients; add to the creamed mixture alternately with the buttermilk. Stir in oats and dates. Pour into an 8 x 4 loaf pan coated with cooking spray. Bake at 350° for 75 minutes or until a toothpick inserted in the center comes out clean. Cool in pan for 10 minutes then remove to a wire rack.

The First Kansas Settlements

The first permanent settlements in Kansas were outposts—Fort Leavenworth (1827), Fort Scott (1842) and Fort Riley (1853). They were established to protect travelers along the Santa Fe and Oregon Trails.

Winnie's
Boston Brown Bread

"My great-grandmother, Winnie Burtis, baked this bread in a special steamer made by her husband. She got the flours from the milling department at Manhattan's Kansas State Agricultural College where she attended school. This recipe has been handed down through five generations of our family."

Kimberly Smith—Leavenworth

1 1/2 cups SWEET MILK
1 1/2 cups SOUR MILK
2 cups INDIAN MEAL (cornmeal)
2 cups RYE FLOUR
1 tsp. BAKING SODA

Pinch of SALT
1 cup MOLASSES
RAISINS (optional)
NUTS (optional)

In a bowl, mix all ingredients. Fill an oiled 46-ounce food can 3/4 full. Cover can with a double thickness of oiled wax paper and secure with a rubber band. Place can on a rack in a deep pot and fill pot with enough boiling water to come to the middle of the can. Cover the pot and steam on low heat for 3 hours. When cool, loosen the bread with a knife moved gently down and around the inside of the can, or remove the opposite end and push the bread out.

 # Sunflower Nut Loaves

National Sunflower Association

1 cup FLOUR
1 cup WHEAT FLOUR
1/3 cup SUGAR
3/4 tsp. BAKING SODA
1/2 tsp. SALT
1/4 cup unsulphured MOLASSES

3/4 cup BUTTERMILK
1 EGG, beaten
1/2 cup RAISINS
1/2 cup SUNFLOWER
   KERNELS

In a mixing bowl, sift together the flours, sugar, baking soda and salt. Blend in molasses, buttermilk and egg and then fold in the raisins and sunflower kernels. Pour mixture into a sprayed 9 x 5 loaf pan. Bake at 350° for one hour.

Pumpkin Bread

"This recipe is from my husband's aunt and is a family favorite. My daughter entered this bread at our county fair and won a ribbon for it!"

Clara M. Ebert—St. George

2 1/2 cups UNBLEACHED FLOUR
1 cup WHOLE-WHEAT FLOUR
2 1/2 cups SUGAR
1/3 cup WHEAT GERM
2 tsp. BAKING SODA
1 1/2 tsp. SALT
1 tsp. ground CLOVES

1 tsp. CINNAMON
1 tsp. NUTMEG
4 EGGS
2/3 cup VEGETABLE OIL
2/3 cup WATER
1 can (16 oz.) PUMPKIN
1 cup chopped RAISINS

In a bowl, combine dry ingredients, mixing well. Beat in eggs, then oil and water. Add pumpkin and raisins; mix well. Grease 2 loaf pans and add batter. Bake for 1 1/2 hours at 325°. Remove from pans; cool on wire rack.

Wheat Thins

"This recipe is from my grandmother Latisha Berg's cookbook, which was given to my father, Joseph Berg, in 1906. In 1930 my parents had a 'dinner stop' for railroad workers in Kansas City where they served meals for 15 cents or less."

Robena I. Asbury—Leavenworth

1 3/4 cups WHOLE-WHEAT
      FLOUR
1 1/2 cups FLOUR
1/3 cup OIL

3/4 tsp. SALT
1 cup WATER
1/4 cup HONEY
SALT or ONION SALT

In a large bowl, mix the flours together. Stir in oil, salt, water and honey. Mix ingredients, kneading as little as possible, until dough is smooth. Roll out dough as thin as possible on an ungreased cookie sheet. Score 'crackers' with a knife and then puncture dough with a fork along the lines. Sprinkle with salt or onion salt. Bake at 350° for 7-10 minutes or until crisp and light brown. Serve with stew or soup.

Strawberry Bread

"This is a quick-bread that I always have ready
for family and guests."

Jo Ann M. Mattison—Morning Mist Bed & Breakfast, Lindsborg

2 EGGS, beaten
1/2 cup OIL
1 pkg. (10 oz.) frozen STRAWBERRIES,
    thawed and drained
1 1/2 cups FLOUR
1 cup SUGAR
1 1/2 tsp. CINNAMON
1/2 tsp. BAKING SODA
1/2 tsp. SALT
1/2 cup chopped NUTS

Preheat oven to 350°. Grease and flour a 9 x 5 loaf pan and set aside. In a small mixing bowl, combine eggs, oil and berries. In a larger bowl, combine dry ingredients and nuts. Add strawberry mixture to dry ingredients and stir just until blended. Pour into a loaf pan; bake 50-60 minutes or until a toothpick inserted into the center comes out clean.

Cheese Bread

"This cheese bread is especially delicious with
spaghetti or lasagna."

Harold Elsasser—Clyde

1 lb. CHEDDAR CHEESE, grated
1 lb. MOZZARELLA, grated
1/4 cup PARMESAN CHEESE
1 Tbsp. GARLIC SALT

1 Tbsp. PARSLEY
MAYONNAISE
1 loaf FRENCH BREAD,
    unsliced

In a large bowl, mix the first five ingredients, then add enough mayonnaise to moisten and hold mixture together. Cut the bread loaf in half, lengthwise. Spread each side generously with cheese mixture. Bake at 350° until cheese is just starting to melt and the edges begin to brown. Slice and serve hot.

Serves 6-8.

Chocolate Cinnamon Rolls

*"This came from my husband's grandmother,
Alma Eisenhauer."*

Susan A. Graham—Morrowville

1 pkg. ACTIVE DRY YEAST
3/4 cup warm WATER
1/4 cup SHORTENING
1/3 cup COCOA
1 tsp. SALT
1/4 cup SUGAR

1 EGG
2 1/4 cups FLOUR
1 1/2 tsp. CINNAMON
3 Tbsp. SUGAR
1 Tbsp. BUTTER, melted
Chopped NUTS

In an electric mixer bowl, dissolve yeast in warm water. Add shortening, cocoa, salt, 1/4 cup sugar, egg and 1 cup of flour; beat 2 minutes on medium speed. Stir in remaining flour; mix well. Scrape sides of bowl, cover with a cloth and let rise about 1 hour. Stir down by beating 25 strokes. Turn soft dough onto a floured board; roll into a 9 x 12 rectangle. Mix cinnamon and 3 tablespoons sugar together. Spread dough with butter; sprinkle with cinnamon and sugar mixture. Roll up, beginning at wide side; pinch edges to seal. Cut into 12 pieces; place in a greased and floured 9 x 9 baking pan. Let rise for 40 minutes. Bake at 375° for 25 minutes. Frost immediately with ***Powdered Sugar Frosting*** then sprinkle with nuts.

Makes 1 dozen rolls.

Powdered Sugar Frosting

2 cups POWDERED SUGAR
2 Tbsp. WATER

1 tsp. VANILLA

Combine all ingredients until smooth.

Did You Know?
● *The helicopter was invented by William Purvis and Charles Wilson of Goodland in 1909.*
● *The ICEE machine, the first frozen carbonated drink machine, was invented by Omar Knedlik of Coffeyville in 1961.*

Desserts

Granny Fry's
Peanut Butter Pie

"This was my mother's pie recipe and a family favorite."

Jacki Cahill—Lansing

2/3 cup SUGAR
2 1/2 Tbsp. CORNSTARCH
1 Tbsp. FLOUR
1/2 tsp. SALT
3 cups MILK

3 EGGS, separated
1/4 cup PEANUT BUTTER
1 Tbsp. MARGARINE
1 (9-inch) baked PIE SHELL

In a medium saucepan, combine sugar, cornstarch, flour and salt. Add milk and cook over medium heat until thickened; remove from heat. In a bowl, beat egg yolks. Gradually add a small amount of the hot sugar mixture to the egg yolks, stir and then add egg yolks to the sugar mixture in saucepan; boil for 1 minute, stirring constantly. Add peanut butter and margarine. Cool and pour into pie shell. Spread **Vanilla Meringue** over filling. Bake at 350° for 12-15 minutes or until golden brown.

Vanilla Meringue

3 EGG WHITES
1/4 tsp. CREAM OF TARTAR

6 Tbsp. SUGAR
1/2 tsp. VANILLA

In a bowl, combine egg whites and cream of tartar and beat until soft peaks form. Beat in sugar, 1 tablespoonful at a time until stiff peaks form then stir in vanilla.

Harvest Pumpkin Brownies

"I love to cook and bake. This is a quick dessert recipe."

Jeanette Urbom—Louisburg

1 can (16 oz.) PUMPKIN
4 EGGS
3/4 cup VEGETABLE OIL
2 tsp. VANILLA
2 cups FLOUR
2 cups SUGAR

1 Tbsp. PUMPKIN PIE SPICE
2 tsp. CINNAMON
2 tsp. BAKING POWDER
1 tsp. BAKING SODA
1/2 tsp. SALT

In a large mixing bowl, beat pumpkin, eggs, oil and vanilla until well-mixed. In another bowl, combine dry ingredients; stir into pumpkin mixture. Pour into a greased 10 x 15 baking pan. Bake at 350° for 20-25 minutes. Cool. Frost brownies with *Cream Cheese Frosting*.

Cream Cheese Frosting

6 Tbsp. BUTTER, softened
1 pkg. (3 oz.) CREAM CHEESE,
    softened
2 Tbsp. MILK

1 tsp. VANILLA
1/8 tsp. SALT
1 1/2 cups POWDERED
    SUGAR

In a bowl, beat the butter, cream cheese, milk, vanilla and salt until smooth; add powdered sugar; mix well.

Lemon Cookies

Judith Campbell—Kansas City

2 cups FLOUR
1 tsp. BAKING POWDER
1/2 tsp. SALT
1/2 cup BUTTER

1 cup SUGAR
1 EGG
1 Tbsp. grated LEMON RIND
1 Tbsp. LEMON JUICE

Sift flour, baking powder and salt. Cream butter and add sugar, egg, lemon rind and juice. Beat until light and fluffy. Stir in dry ingredients until completely mixed. Wrap dough in plastic and chill in refrigerator. Roll out dough to 1/8-inch thickness on a lightly floured board. Cut out cookies and place them on an ungreased baking sheet. Sprinkle with sugar and bake in a 375° oven until lightly browned (6-8 minutes).

Mom Flory's Taffy

"This is a fun tradition we enjoyed with our grandparents (we called them 'Mom' and 'Pop'). They would make the taffy and we would all take turns pulling it."

Lawanda J. Gorton—Ottawa

2 cups SUGAR	3 Tbsp. BUTTER
Pinch of SALT	1 tsp. VANILLA
1 cup LIGHT CORN SYRUP	1/4 tsp. FOOD COLORING
3/4 cup WATER	(optional)

In a heavy 3-quart pan, mix sugar, salt, corn syrup and water; add butter. Stir constantly over moderate heat until mixture comes to a boil. Cook without stirring until mixture reaches 260° F on a candy thermometer or until a small amount forms a hard ball when dropped into cold water. Stir in vanilla and coloring. Pour into a greased 9-inch pan; let stand for 20 minutes or until mixture is cool enough to handle. Butter hands; pick up taffy in one piece (2 people); pull about 2-3 feet, fold over and continue pulling and folding until it gets creamy and stiff. Pull into 1/2-inch rope, twisting while you pull. Cut into 1-inch pieces; wrap pieces in plastic wrap or waxed paper. Store in an airtight container.

Rhubarb Pie

"This recipe came from my mother-in-law. It was her favorite pie to bake in the spring when she had fresh rhubarb. It's like a custard and very delicious."

Madonna Sorell—Rustic Remembrances Bed & Breakfast, Glasco

2 cups chopped RHUBARB	1 cup MILK
1 (9-inch) unbaked PIE SHELL	2 Tbsp. FLOUR
1 cup SUGAR	1/2 tsp. SALT
2 EGGS, beaten	2 Tbsp. BUTTER, softened

Spread rhubarb in pie shell. In a bowl, whip together the remaining ingredients; pour over rhubarb. Bake at 350° for 45 minutes or until a toothpick placed in the center comes out clean.

Springerle Cookies
(German Christmas cookies)

"When I was a child, Springerle Cookies were always made several weeks before Christmas. A special rolling pin with notched-out patterns and cutting lines was used. As they age the flavor improves. They continue to be a family tradition."

Nola Elsasser—Clyde

6 EGGS	2 tsp. BAKING POWDER
1 tsp. SALT	6-7 cups FLOUR
3 cups SUGAR	1-2 tsp. ANISE OIL
1 tsp. BAKING SODA	ANISE SEEDS

In a large mixing bowl, beat eggs until very foamy; add salt and beat again. Slowly add the sugar and beat for 10 minutes. In another bowl, sift together baking soda, baking powder and 3 cups of the flour; add to egg and sugar mixture. Combine 2 cups of the remaining flour and anise oil and add to mixture. Let stand for 30 minutes to thicken. Sift 1-2 cups of flour to work into dough while rolling out. Roll dough out on a floured surface to a 1/4-inch thickness and cut out cookies; set them on waxed paper to dry overnight. Just before baking, press an anise seed under each cookie and place them on a greased cookie sheet. Bake at 340° for 10 minutes or until light brown.

Rice Custard

"This has been a family favorite for many years!"

Shirley Atkinson—Wichita

6 EGGS	1/2 tsp. SALT
3 cups MILK	1 1/2 cups COOKED RICE
1 cup SUGAR	1 cup GOLDEN RAISINS
1 tsp. VANILLA	

Place eggs in a buttered casserole dish and beat lightly with a fork. Add milk, sugar, vanilla and salt; blend well. Stir in rice and raisins. Set casserole in a pan of water and bake, uncovered, for 1 1/4 hours at 350°, stirring once after the first half hour.

Old-Fashioned Molasses Cookies

"These are very much like my grandmother's molasses cookies. She always had these soft, round cookies for munching when I came to spend the summer with her."

Marian Geist—Hays

3/4 cup BUTTER,
    melted and cooled
1 cup SUGAR
1/4 cup UNSULPHURED
    MOLASSES
1 lg. EGG, beaten

2 cups ALL-PURPOSE FLOUR
1 tsp. BAKING SODA
1/2 tsp. ground CLOVES
3/4 tsp. GINGER
3/4 tsp. CINNAMON
1/2 tsp. SALT

In a medium mixing bowl, combine butter, 1/2 cup sugar, molasses and egg; mix well by hand. In another mixing bowl, sift together the flour, baking soda, cloves, ginger, cinnamon and salt. Stir dry mixture into creamed mixture (the dough will be soft and sticky). Cover dough and chill for several hours. When ready to bake, preheat oven to 375°. Roll small portions of dough into 1-inch balls then roll each ball in remaining sugar to coat. Place balls 2-inches apart on cookie sheets and bake for 8-10 minutes. Remove from oven; let cookies cool on sheets for 1 minute then remove to cool completely. Store in an airtight container.

Overland Park

Overland Park is one of the largest cities in the state and the leading business and commercial center for the Johnson County portion of the Kansas City metropolitan area. This city boasts a thriving hospitality industry, hosting over 1.5 million in 1999. The NCAA Visitors Center provides a photographic and videotape tribute to intercollegiate athletics and represents all 21 NCAA sports as well as the national champions.

Apple-Raspberry Crisp

"My grandma and mom always loved cobblers and crisps. This is one of the many recipes they handed down to me."

Pat Habiger—Spearville

1/4 cup MARGARINE, softened	1 pkg. (10 oz.) frozen
1/4 cup QUICK-COOKING OATS	RASPBERRIES thawed
1/4 cup FLOUR	2 tsp. LEMON JUICE
1/4 cup packed BROWN SUGAR	1/2 tsp. VANILLA
1 lg. APPLE, peeled and sliced	1/2 tsp. CINNAMON

In a bowl, combine margarine, oats, flour and brown sugar; mix until crumbly then set aside. In a medium bowl, combine apple, drained raspberries, lemon juice, vanilla and cinnamon. Toss to coat fruit. Pour into a greased 8 x 10 baking dish. Spoon oat mixture evenly on top. Bake at 400° for 15-20 minutes.

Serves 4.

Pineapple Delight

"This recipe is for a dessert my grandmother often made for family dinners and special occasions. The whipping cream she used was genuine cream from their milk cows."

Anita Fassnacht—Muscotah

1/2 lb. MARSHMALLOWS
1/2 cup MILK
1 cup WHIPPING CREAM
1 cup crushed PINEAPPLE, drained
2 cups GRAHAM CRACKER CRUMBS
1/2 cup BUTTER, melted

In a small saucepan, combine marshmallows and milk and heat until marshmallows have melted; let cool. In a separate bowl, whip cream then add pineapple and marshmallow mixture. Mix graham cracker crumbs with butter and spread in an 8 x 10 baking dish. Pour marshmallow mixture over crumbs and sprinkle top with additional crumbs. Chill at least 24 hours.

Serves 6.

Note: Any fruit can be used in place of the pineapple.

Grandma's Eggnog Pie

"This recipe came from my mother-in-law's mother, Mary Jane Bishop. She lived on a farm north of Belle Plain and often made this pie for the harvest crew."

Shirley A. Shipman—Belle Plaine

1 Tbsp. unflavored GELATIN	1/2 cup SUGAR
1 1/2 cups COLD MILK	1 tsp. VANILLA
3 EGGS, separated	1 cup HEAVY CREAM, whipped
1/4 tsp. NUTMEG	1 (9-inch) baked PIE SHELL
1/4 tsp. SALT	NUTMEG

In a small bowl, soften gelatin in 1/4 cup of the milk. In a double-boiler, heat the remaining milk to scalding; remove from heat. In a mixing bowl, beat egg yolks, nutmeg, salt and sugar; slowly add the scalded milk, stirring constantly. Return to double-boiler and cook until mixture thickens and can coat a spoon; stir in softened gelatin until it dissolves. Chill. When mixture begins to thicken, fold in stiffly beaten egg whites and vanilla then fold in whipped cream. Pour into pie shell; chill until firm. Sprinkle with nutmeg.

Baked Custard Cups

"My great-grandmother, Winnie Burtis, came to Kansas in a covered wagon in 1868. She often made this custard. I inherited her set of custard cups."

Kimberly Smith—Leavenworth

3 EGGS, slightly beaten	1 tsp. VANILLA
1/3 cup SUGAR	2 1/2 cups MILK, scalded
Dash of SALT	NUTMEG

Preheat oven to 350°. In a bowl, blend eggs, sugar, salt and vanilla; gradually stir in milk. Pour into six (6-ounce) custard cups and sprinkle with nutmeg. Place cups in a 9 x 13 baking pan then pour very hot water into pan to within 1/2-inch of tops of cups. Bake 45 minutes or until knife inserted halfway between center and edge comes out clean. Serve warm or cold.

Lemon Fluff

*"This is a very old recipe from my mother. It is one
of my family's favorites."*

Jessie R. Davis—Canton

1 can (13 oz.) EVAPORATED MILK
1 pkg. (3 oz.) LEMON GELATIN
1 cup boiling WATER
1 pkg. (3 oz.) CREAM CHEESE, softened
1 cup SUGAR
1 tsp. VANILLA
20 GRAHAM CRACKERS, finely crushed
2 Tbsp. SUGAR
1/2 cup MARGARINE, melted

Pour evaporated milk into ice cube trays and chill until
crystals form 1/2-inch from edge. In a small bowl, dissolve gelatin
in boiling water then cool until it starts to set. In another bowl,
whip together cream cheese, sugar and vanilla. In a mixing bowl,
whip chilled milk until peaks form. Add gelatin mixture and
cream cheese mixture to whipped milk and whip thoroughly. Mix
graham cracker crumbs, sugar and margarine. Spread 1/2 of the
crumbs in a 9 x 13 baking dish. Spread lemon mixture on top;
sprinkle with remaining crumbs and chill.

Note: For best flavor, prepare a day ahead and refrigerate.

Council Grove

*In the summer of 1825, Osage Indian chiefs
and U.S. commissioners signed an agree-
ment that gave the government the right-of-way for the
Santa Fe Trail as well as the name for this town on the
Neosho River. The remains of Council Oak, under which
the agreement was signed, are enshrined there. Post Office
Oak, a tree a short distance away, served
as an unofficial post office—1825-1847.
Letters were left in a stone cache at its foot
to be picked up by the next wagon train.*

Sour Cream Chocolate Cake

Bonnie Niles—Arkansas City

2 cups FLOUR
2 cups SUGAR
1 1/4 tsp. BAKING SODA
1/2 tsp. BAKING POWDER
2 EGGS
3/4 cup SOUR CREAM

1/4 cup SHORTENING
1 cup WATER
1 tsp. VANILLA
4 oz. UNSWEETENED
    CHOCOLATE, melted

In a mixing bowl, sift dry ingredients together. In a large mixing bowl, mix together the eggs, sour cream, shortening, water, vanilla and chocolate. Beat well. Add dry ingredients to creamed mixture and beat well. Grease and flour a 9 x 13 baking pan then add batter. Bake at 350° for 40 minutes. Spread *Chocolate Butter Frosting* on cake after it has cooled.

Chocolate Butter Frosting

1/3 cup BUTTER, softened
3 oz. UNSWEETENED
    CHOCOLATE, melted

3 cups POWDERED SUGAR
1/2 cup SOUR CREAM
2 tsp. VANILLA

In a medium mixing bowl, combine all ingredients; beat until smooth.

Peanut Butter Ice Cream

"This is a favorite with ice cream lovers!"

Gloria J. Moore—Gloria's Coffee and Quilts, Barnes

4 lg. EGGS
2 cups SUGAR
2 cups chunky PEANUT BUTTER
2 cups CREAM

2 Tbsp. VANILLA
1/2 tsp. SALT
2-3 qts. MILK

In a large bowl, beat eggs until frothy. Mix in sugar and peanut butter. Add cream, vanilla and salt to mixture; blend well. Pour into a 1-gallon ice cream freezer. Fill container to fill line with milk and freeze per freezer directions.

Yellow Brick Road Cake

"This is a great recipe for a quick and especially good-tasting dessert. There's 'no place like home' Kansas cooking."

Alexa Berman—Overland Park

1 box (18.25 oz.) PINEAPPLE CAKE MIX
3/4 cup WATER
1/3 cup RUM
3 EGGS
1 sm. BANANA, mashed
1/2 cup crushed PINEAPPLE, drained
1/2 cup shredded COCONUT
1 can (16 oz.) CREAM CHEESE FROSTING

Preheat oven to 350°. Blend cake mix, water, rum and eggs in a large mixer bowl; mix at low speed until moistened. Add banana, pineapple and coconut.; blend at medium speed for 2 minutes. Pour batter into a greased sheet cake pan. Bake for 30-40 minutes or until a toothpick inserted in the center comes out clean. Cool completely; frost with cream cheese frosting.

Sweet Potato Pie

"This is my idea of a good sweet potato pie. I often make it for special dinners."

Opal Nicholson—Kansas City

3 EGGS
1 1/2 cups SUGAR
1 1/2 tsp. VANILLA
1 1/2 cups mashed SWEET POTATOES
1 lg. can (14 oz.) SWEETENED CONDENSED MILK
1/2 stick MARGARINE, melted
1 (10-inch) unbaked PIE SHELL
NUTMEG

In a medium mixing bowl, beat eggs then add the next five ingredients and mix well. Pour into pie shell and sprinkle top with nutmeg. Bake at 450° for 10 minutes then reduce temperature to 350° and bake another 10-20 minutes or until firm.

Almond-Coconut Cake

"This recipe was given to me by my niece who usually brings this dessert to our family reunions."

Eleanor Penka—Healy

1 pkg. (18.25 oz.) DEVIL'S FOOD CAKE MIX

Prepare cake mix according to package directions. Pour into 2 greased and floured 9 x 13 cake pans. Bake at 350° for 20 minutes. When cake has cooled cover it evenly with *Marshmallow Spread* and drizzle with *Chocolate Chip Topping*.

Marshmallow Spread

1 cup EVAPORATED MILK
1 cup SUGAR
24 lg. MARSHMALLOWS

1 bag (14 oz.) shredded
COCONUT

Mix milk and sugar in a medium sauce pan and bring to a rapid boil. Remove from heat and add marshmallows. Stir mixture until marshmallows have melted then stir in coconut.

Chocolate Chip Topping

1 1/2 cups SUGAR
1 stick MARGARINE
1/2 cup EVAPORATED MILK

1 1/2 cups CHOCOLATE
CHIPS
3/4 cup chopped ALMONDS

Combine sugar, margarine and milk and heat to a rolling boil. Remove from heat and add chocolate chips, stirring until melted. Fold in almonds.

Abilene

Abilene's reputation as "the wildest town in the West" grew, along with the city, as hundreds of cowboys who traveled the Chisholm Trail came to town. Wild Bill Hickok, a legendary gunslinger, was the marshal here in 1871. Abilene was also the boyhood home of Dwight D. Eisenhower, the 34th president of the United States.

Raisin Pudding

"My mother gave me this vintage recipe, and I used it a lot when I cooked for harvest crews because I could put it together quickly and cook it early in the morning."

Elaine Clark—Wellington

2 cups boiling WATER
1 1/2 cups SUGAR
2 Tbsp. BUTTER
1 tsp. VANILLA
1 cup FLOUR
3 tsp. BAKING POWDER

1/2 cup packed BROWN
   SUGAR
1/2 tsp. CINNAMON
1/8 tsp. SALT
3/4 cup RAISINS
3/4 cup MILK

In a 9 x 13 baking dish, mix together the boiling water, 1 cup sugar, butter and vanilla. Stir until the sugar and butter are dissolved. In a separate bowl, mix the flour, baking powder, remaining 1/2 cup sugar, brown sugar, cinnamon and salt. Add raisins and milk; blend until the batter is smooth. Pour over mixture in baking dish. Bake at 350° for 45-50 minutes.

Serves 12-15.

Banana Cake

"An original recipe that has become a family favorite."

Letty Wasserman—Overland Park

3 EGGS, separated
1/2 cup BUTTER, softened
1 1/2 cups SUGAR
1 cup mashed BANANAS
1 tsp. VANILLA
3 cups FLOUR

1 tsp. BAKING SODA
3 tsp. BAKING POWDER
1 cup SOUR CREAM
1 can (16 oz.) CHOCOLATE
   FROSTING

In a small bowl, beat egg whites until stiff; set aside. In a mixing bowl, cream together butter and sugar. Add egg yolks, bananas and vanilla. Combine flour, baking soda and baking powder and add alternately with sour cream to creamed mixture. Fold in egg whites. Pour into a greased 9 x 13 baking pan. Bake at 350° for 30 minutes. When cool, frost with chocolate frosting.

Elderberry Pie

"This is an original recipe from the 1930s that my grandmother gave to me."

Kitty Borg—Alta Vista

1/2 cup FLOUR
1 1/2 cups SUGAR
1/4 cup VINEGAR
1 3/4 cups ELDERBERRIES

1 3/4 cups sliced APPLES
2 (9-inch) unbaked PIE
 CRUSTS
1 Tbsp. BUTTER

In a medium bowl, mix flour, sugar, vinegar, elderberries, and apples. Pour into bottom crust, dot with butter and add top crust. Pinch edges to seal and pierce top with tines of a fork. Bake at 425° for 10 minutes then reduce temperature to 350° and bake for 30 minutes.

Greetings!

Hallmark Cards, the largest greeting card company in the world, is headquartered in Kansas City, Missouri. The company operates plants in Topeka, Lawrence and Leavenworth.

Mahogany Cake

"This is a family favorite."

Shirley Anne Jones—Hanover

1/2 cup SHORTENING
2 cups SUGAR
2 EGGS, well-beaten
2 1/2 cups ALL-PURPOSE
 FLOUR
2 tsp. BAKING SODA

1 tsp. SALT
1 cup MILK
6 Tbsp. COCOA
1 cup hot WATER
1 tsp. VANILLA

In a large mixing bowl, cream together shortening and sugar; add eggs. In a separate bowl, sift together flour, baking soda and salt; add alternately with the milk to the creamed mixture. Combine cocoa, vanilla and water and add to mixture. Pour into a greased and floured 9 x 13 baking pan. Bake at 375° for 30-35 minutes. Cool and frost with your favorite frosting.

Ranger Cookies

"My grandmother often made these big cookies for us."

Betty Harlow—Gardner

1 cup SUGAR
1 cup packed BROWN SUGAR
1 cup SHORTENING
2 EGGS, beaten
1 tsp. VANILLA
1/2 tsp. BAKING POWDER
1 tsp. BAKING SODA

1/2 tsp. SALT
2 cups FLOUR
2 cups QUICK-COOKING
   OATMEAL
2 cups WHEAT FLAKES
1 cup shredded COCONUT
1 cup chopped NUTS

In a large mixing bowl, cream sugars and shortening until light and fluffy then stir in eggs and vanilla. Sift baking powder, baking soda, salt and flour; add to creamed mixture and stir well. Mix in remaining ingredients; mix. Drop by tablespoonfuls onto a baking sheet and press flat with a fork that has been dipped in water. Bake at 375° for 15 minutes or until light brown.

 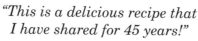 # Christmas Divinity

*"This is a delicious recipe that
I have shared for 45 years!"*

Helen Cloke—Chanute

3/4 cup LIGHT CORN SYRUP
3 cups SUGAR
3/4 cup WATER
2 EGG WHITES
1 pkg. (1 oz.) unflavored
   GELATIN

1 cup chopped NUTS
1/2 cup shredded COCONUT
1 tsp. VANILLA
Dash of SALT

In a medium saucepan, mix corn syrup, sugar and water; heat to boiling point. Reduce heat and cook until a few drops tested in cold water form a hard ball. Beat egg whites until they begin to fluff up. Add dry gelatin to egg whites and beat until mixture forms stiff points. Continue to beat while pouring in a thin stream of the syrup mixture. Stir in remaining ingredients. Pour into a buttered pan. Chill until firm.

Botkin Raisin Cookies

"My aunt, Bertha Botkin, created this family recipe years ago. Aunt Bert was like a mother to my mom, Clara Smith; and they both were excellent cooks!"

Carol Foy—Arkansas City

1 cup RAISINS
1 cup SUGAR
1 stick MARGARINE, softened
2 EGGS, beaten
2 cups FLOUR, sifted
1/2 tsp. BAKING SODA

1/2 tsp. SALT
1/2 tsp. CINNAMON
1/2 tsp. NUTMEG
1/2 tsp. ALLSPICE
1 cup chopped NUTS

In a small saucepan, cover raisins with water and cook until plump; strain, reserving liquid, then cool. In a mixing bowl, cream sugar, margarine and eggs. Sift flour, baking soda, salt and spices into a bowl and add to the creamed mixture. Fold in raisins and nuts. If dough seems too stiff or dry, add a little raisin water. Drop dough by tablespoonfuls onto a cookie sheet. Bake at 375° for 10-15 minutes or until brown.

Makes about 5 dozen cookies.

Mom's  Pecan Pie

"This recipe is very easy to make and quite delicious."

Anna M. Landauer—Basehor

3 EGGS
1 cup CORN SYRUP
1/2 cup SUGAR
1 tsp. VANILLA

2 Tbsp. BUTTER, melted
1/8 tsp. SALT
1 cup chopped PECANS
1 (9-inch) unbaked PIE SHELL

In a medium mixing bowl, beat eggs lightly then stir in corn syrup, sugar, vanilla, butter and salt. Add pecans and mix well. Pour into pie shell. Cover edges of pie loosely with foil. Bake at 350° for 20 minutes; remove foil and continue baking for 20 minutes or until knife inserted in center comes out clean.

Bill Hogue's Apple Goodie

"This hearty dessert is requested at all of our family gatherings at the ranch."

Bill and Kathy Hogue—Mission Valley Ranch, Topeka

Syrup:
- 1 1/2 cups SUGAR
- 1 1/2 cups WATER
- 1/4 tsp. CINNAMON
- 1/4 tsp. NUTMEG
- 6-10 drops RED FOOD COLORING

Dough:
- 3 Tbsp. BUTTER
- 2 cups ALL-PURPOSE FLOUR
- 2 tsp. BAKING POWDER
- 1 tsp. SALT
- 2/3 cup SHORTENING
- 1/2 cup MILK

6 med. APPLES, pared and sliced
CINNAMON
SUGAR

In a medium saucepan, combine sugar, water, cinnamon, nutmeg and food coloring; bring to a boil. Remove from heat and add butter. In a large mixing bowl, sift together dry ingredients; cut in shortening until mixture resembles coarse crumbs. Add milk, stirring just until flour is moistened. On a lightly floured surface, roll dough out into a 1/4-inch thick rectangle. Cut out a solid piece to fit a 9 x 13 glass baking dish. Cut remaining dough into 1/2-inch strips. Place apples over dough in baking dish and criss-cross top with dough strips. Cover with syrup mixture and generously sprinkle with cinnamon and sugar. Bake at 375° for 50-55 minutes.

Topeka

Topeka was founded in 1854 and incorporated in 1857, with Cyrus K. Holliday, the founder of the Atchison, Topeka & Santa Fe Railway, as mayor. Topeka became the state capital in 1861. Today, it is the fourth largest city in Kansas and home to the world-famous Menninger Foundation, Washburn University and historic Ward-Meade Park.

Grandma's Raisin Pie

"This recipe came from my grandmother. She loved to make this pie for family reunions and gatherings. I often make it for my family."

Theresa A. Smith—Erie

1 cup RAISINS	1 EGG, beaten
2 cups warm WATER	1 Tbsp. BUTTER
3 1/2 Tbsp. FLOUR or TAPIOCA	2 Tbsp. LEMON JUICE
1/2 cup SUGAR	1 Tbsp. grated LEMON PEEL
1/2 tsp. SALT	1 (9-inch) unbaked PIE SHELL

In a saucepan, cover raisins with water; cover pan and simmer for 30 minutes. Drain and measure liquid. Add enough water to make 2 cups . In a large mixing bowl, combine flour or tapioca, sugar, salt and raisin liquid. Add mixture to raisins in saucepan and cook on medium heat until thickened, stirring constantly. Pour a small amount of the hot mixture into beaten egg and mix well. Add egg mixture to raisin mixture and bring to a boil. Remove from heat, add butter, lemon juice and grated peel and stir. Pour mixture into pie shell and bake at 350° for 20-30 minutes.

Mother's Applesauce Cake

"I remember Mother making this cake when I was a little girl. She is 98 years young now so this is a 'good old recipe'."

Marva Lee Doud—Salina

1 cup BUTTER, softened	1 tsp. CINNAMON
2 cups SUGAR	1/4 tsp. ground CLOVES
2 cups APPLESAUCE	1/4 tsp. NUTMEG
3 1/2 cups FLOUR	1 cup chopped NUTS
2 tsp. BAKING SODA	1 cup GOLDEN RAISINS

In a large mixing bowl, cream together butter and sugar; stir in applesauce. In a separate bowl, sift together dry ingredients. Mix dry ingredients into creamed mixture and add nuts and raisins. Pour batter into a greased and floured tube pan. Bake at 350° for 45-60 minutes.

Frosted Sugar Cookies

"These cookies are my family's favorite."

Ozetta Elley—Kansas City

1 cup BUTTER, softened	2 1/2 cups FLOUR
1 1/2 cups POWDERED SUGAR	1 tsp. BAKING SODA
1 EGG, beaten	1 tsp. CREAM OF TARTAR
1 tsp. VANILLA	1/2 tsp. SALT
1/2 tsp. ALMOND EXTRACT	

In a large mixing bowl, cream together butter and sugar until fluffy. Mix in egg and flavorings. In a separate bowl, sift together flour, baking soda, cream of tartar and salt. Mix dry ingredients, a little at a time, into creamed mixture. Cover and refrigerate 3-4 hours (or overnight). When ready to bake, preheat oven to 350°. Divide dough in half; roll out on a lightly floured surface to 3/8-inch thickness. Using cookie cutters, cut dough into shapes. Place on a baking sheet and bake 7-10 minutes or until light brown on edges. Remove from oven; let set 2-3 minutes before removing to wire rack to cool. Frost with *Powdered Sugar Frosting* and decorate as desired.

Yields 4 dozen.

Powdered Sugar Frosting

1/3 cup BUTTER or MARGARINE, softened
3 cups POWDERED SUGAR
1 tsp. VANILLA
2 Tbsp. MILK or CREAM

In a medium mixing bowl, combine butter, powdered sugar, vanilla and milk. Beat until smooth and creamy.

Cheyenne Bottoms

A 60-square mile area of wetlands north of the Arkansas River near Great Bend—serves as a "hotel" for millions of migrating birds each spring and fall, including almost half of the North American shorebird population.

Raisin Spice Bars

"This recipe was given to me by my sister."

Maxine Cuppet—Savonburg

1 cup RAISINS	1 cup SUGAR
1/2 cup SHORTENING	1 tsp. CINNAMON
1/2 tsp. BAKING SODA	1/2 tsp. ground CLOVES
2 cups FLOUR	1/4 tsp. SALT

In a small saucepan, cook raisins with enough water to make 1 cup of juice. Strain; set raisins aside, reserving juice. In a mixing bowl, blend shortening, baking soda and the hot juice. Combine flour, sugar, cinnamon, cloves and salt; add to juice mixture. Blend in raisins. Spread dough on a greased cookie sheet. Bake at 375° for 25 minutes. Cool. Either frost with **Powdered Sugar Frosting** (see page 86) or leave plain. Cut into squares to serve.

Whole-Wheat Sugar Cookies

Kansas Wheat Commission—Manhattan

1 cup SUGAR	1/2 tsp. BAKING SODA
1/2 cup BUTTER, softened	1/2 tsp. SALT
1 EGG	1/2 tsp. ground NUTMEG
2 Tbsp. MILK	1 Tbsp. grated ORANGE PEEL
1 tsp. VANILLA	1/2 tsp. CINNAMON
2 cups WHOLE-WHEAT FLOUR	2 tsp. SUGAR
1 tsp. BAKING POWDER	

Preheat oven to 375°. On medium speed of an electric mixer, cream sugar and butter until light and fluffy, about 5 minutes. Add egg, milk and vanilla; beat well. Combine flour, baking powder, baking soda, salt, nutmeg and orange peel; gradually add to creamed mixture, mixing until blended. In a small bowl, combine cinnamon and sugar. Shape dough into 1-inch balls. Flatten with the bottom of a dampened glass dipped in the cinnamon-sugar mixture. Place 2-inches apart on cookie sheets coated with cooking spray. Bake for 9 to 10 minutes or until lightly browned. Cool on wire racks.

Kansas Food Festivals

*The following is a partial listing of the food-related events held throughout Kansas
each year. Contact local Chambers of Commerce or Tourist Information Bureaus
for a complete listing of all events.*

March
International Pancake Day, Liberal
April
Mennonite Relief Sale, Hutchinson
Outdoor Redbud Festival, Kechi
May
Cinco de Mayo, Hutchinson
Haskell Indian Pow Wow, Lawrence
Millfest, Lindsborg
Koester Museum BBQ, Marysville
Spring Fling, Chetopa
Frontier Days BBQ, Abbyville
Americana Weekend, Kansas City
Cherry Blossom Festival, Cherryvale
Celebration of Cultures, Topeka
Folk Festival, Hillsboro
June
German Fest, Marysville
Prairie Days, Canton
Smokey Hill River Festival, Salina
City Celebration, Almena
Annual BBQ, Morrowville
Pottawatomi Pow Wow, Mayetta
Scottish Highland Games, Kansas City
Jayhawker Days, Ottawa
Juneteenth, Great Bend
Midsummer's Day Festival, Lindsborg
BBQ Battle and Championship, Lenexa
St. John's Mexican Fiesta, Lawrence
Territorial Capital Festival, Lecompton
Chisholm Trail Festival, Newton
July
Spirit of Kansas, Topeka
4th of July Celebration, Gridley
Play Day in the Park, Salina
Kansas Wheat Festival, Wellington
Pomona Days, Ottawa
Bluegrass Festival, Colby
Fiesta Mexicana Week, Topeka
Saddle Club Rodeo, Attica
Frontier Days, Haddam
August
Threshing Days, Goessel
Sunflower Festival, Goodland

Flint Hills Beef Fest, Emporia
Pride of Hoyt Days, Hoyt
State Fiddling Championships, Lawrence
Yoder Heritage Day, Hutchinson
Pony Express Festival, Hanover
Little Balkans Days, Pittsburg
September
Lake Shawnee Pow Wow, Topeka
Railroad Days, Topeka
Fiesta, Emporia
Labor Day Celebration, Milford
Watermelon Festival, Clyde
Labor Day Celebration, Kiowa
Spinach & Trails Festival, Lenexa
Teddy Bear Picnic, Wichita
Mexican Fiesta, Garden City
Autumn Gold Parade, Kansas City
Cider Days, Topeka
Circlefest, Circleville
Fall Fest, Condordia
Grinter Applefest, Kansas City
Little Apple Festival, Manhattan
Multicultural Festival, Great Bend
Santa Fe Days, Salina
Scottish Festival, McPherson
Octoberfest, Hays
Old Settler's Day, Marion
October
Apple Festival, Topeka
Great Grillers BBQ "Meat", Shawnee
Chili Cook-off, Hutchinson
Homecoming Festival, Fredonia
Fun Day, Glasco
Corn Show, Jewell
Polka Fest, Paxico
Chili Challenge, Lenexa
Peddlers Market, Ellinwood
November
Intertribal Pow Wow, Coffeyville
Veteran's Day Celebration, Iola
December
Holidays in Wellsville, Wellsville
Santa's Gifts & Goodies, Washington
Xmas Candy & Bake Sale, Junction City

Index

Index (continued)

Index (continued)

Recipe Contributors

Bunny Adams—Atwood 54
G. Anderson—LandMark Inn, Oberlin 22, 59
Karen Anderson, Wichita 34
Lucinda Anstaett—Newton 52
Robena I. Asbury—Leavenworth 66
Shirley Atkinson—Wichita 72
Diane Balanoff—Leawood 10, 51
Polly R. Bales—Logan 35
Merry Barker—Flint Hills B&B, Council Grove 20
Howard & Anna Beck—Hesston 8, 21, 26, 31
Midge Befort—Kansas City 29
Alexa Berman—Overland Park 78
Marion Bogart—Kensington 14, 48, 51
Kitty Borg—Alta Vista 81
Jacki Cahill—Lansing 28, 57, 69
Judith Campbell—Kansas City 70
Mary Carson—Quenemo 45
Esther Clapham—Larned 43
Elaine Clark—Wellington 21, 80
Wendy Clasten—Leawood 55
Helen Cloke—Chanute 82
Leon "Butch" Cuppet—Savonburg 14, 41
Maxine Cuppet—Savonburg 87
Nancy Darish—Overland Park 50
Ardie A. Davis, Mission 11
Jessie R. Davis—Canton 76
Joan Donahue—Clover Cliff B&B, Elmdale 20
Marva Lee Doud—Salina 41, 85
Clara M. Ebert—St. George 66
L. Ediger—Wrought Iron Inn B&B, Hutchinson 17
Ozetta Elley—Kansas City 86
Harold Elsasser—Clyde 67
Nola Elsasser—Clyde 72
Anita Fassnacht—Muscotah 74
Judith Fertig—Overland Park 38
Cindy Flax—Hays 55
Carol Foy—Arkansas City 83
Margaret Gaskell—Horton 28
Marian Geist—Hays 73
Marilyn Gordon—Topeka 26
Lawanda J. Gorton—Ottawa 15, 18, 71
Susan A. Graham—Morrowville 68
Debby Greenstein—Overland Park 36, 56
Belle Grimsley—Americus 44, 62
Pat Habiger—Spearville 46, 74
Betty Harlow—Gardner 82
Laura K. Hicks—Lansing 32
Teresa J. Hicks—Lansing 40

Melissa A. Hicks—Lansing 63
Deborah Hill—Coffeyville 9
Bill & Kathy Hogue—Mission Valley Ranch, Topeka 42, 84
K. Holt—Cimarron Hotel, Cimarron 7, 9, 48
Joyce M. Jandera—Hanover 8, 33
Shirley Anne Jones—Hanover 81
Sandy Lundgren—Olathe 27, 30
Marci Kellner—Stilwell 58
Mildred P. Kinder—Leavenworth 56
Paul Kirk—Roeland Park 37, 39
Anna M. Landauer—Basehor 83
Sally Lundgren, Olathe 27, 30
P. Lyons—Lyons' House B&B, Fort Scott 12, 23
Jo Ann Mattison—Morning Mist B&B 67
Miller's 101 Ranch—Kinsley 60-61
G. Moore—Gloria's Coffee & Quilts, Barnes 77
N. Newman—Country Reflections B&B, Holton 15
Opal Nicholson—Kansas City 78
Bonnie Niles—Arkansas City 77
R. Nitzel—Peaceful Acres B&B, Great Bend 19
Edna Ohlsen—Horton 58
Martha Sue Olander—Linwood 49
Scott O'Meara, Overland Park 10
Twila Pearson—Hoxie 17
Eleanor Penka—Healy 79
A. Petrik—Wind, Earth & Sky, Caldwell 31, 53
Anita Phillips—Great Bend 45
Merrill Powers—Spearville 64
Geneva Pryce—Newton 62
M. Reese—Creek Side Farm, Fowler 13, 47
Susan Rosenthal—Leawood 59
Rose Schukman—Hays 24
Shirley A. Shipman—Belle Plaine 75
Guy Simpson—Shawnee 39
Kimberly Smith—Leavenworth 65, 75
Theresa A. Smith—Erie 85
Madonna Sorell, Rustic Remembrances Bed & Breakfast, Glasco 71
B. Stoecklein—Plumb House B&B, Emporia 18
Maralee Thompson—Lansing 16
Jeanette Urbom—Louisburg 70
Charlene M. Wagner—Easton 32, 36
Letty Wasserman—Overland Park 46, 80
Alberta C. Welch—Rapid City 43
Frances Wienck—Barnes 54
Tina Woolley—Smoky Valley B&B, Lindsborg 12
Linda Zack—Leawood 30

COLORADO COOK BOOK

Bring a taste of Colorado to your dinner table! Sample fishermen's fillets, gold miners' stews, Native American and Southwestern favorites, vegetarian feasts and skiers' hot toddies! Recipes, facts and folklore about Colorado.

5 1/2 x 8 1/2 — 128 pages . . . $6.95

OKLAHOMA COOK BOOK

A roundup of delicious recipes captures the rich cultural and historical charm of Oklahoma. Traditional and contemporary recipes from *Panhandle Pancakes* and *Cowboy Fajitas* to *Chicken Fried Steak* and *Fried Green Tomatoes*.

5 1/2 x 8 1/2 — 96 pages . . . $6.95

ILLINOIS COOK BOOK

Enjoy the flavors of Illinois! Over 100 recipes that celebrate Illinois. *Reuben in the Round, Pork Medallions in Herb Sauce, Autumn's Swiss Supper, Carrot Soufflé, Sky High Honey Biscuits, Rhubarb Cream Pie* to name just a few. Includes fascinating facts and trivia.

5 1/2 x 8 1/2 — 96 pages . . . $6.95

IOWA COOK BOOK

Recipes from across America's heartland. From *Indian Two-Corn Pudding* to *Pork Chops Braised in White Wine* this cookbook presents home-grown favorites and encompasses both ethnic traditions and gourmet specialties. A special section entitled "Iowa Corn Recipes" highlights this state's most famous export.

5 1/2 x 8 1/2 — 96 pages . . . $6.95

TEXAS COOK BOOK

Over 200 Tasty Texas Recipes and a side of Texas Trivia, too! Chili, barbecue, cowboy, Tex-Mex, stir-fry and many more favorite recipes submitted by Texans make this book a treat in any state. Learn about Texas traditions and history as you sample the best of Texas!

5 1/2 x 8 1/2 —144 pages . . . $5.95

CORN LOVERS COOK BOOK

Over 100 delicious recipes featuring America's favorite! Try *Corn Chowder, Corn Soufflé, Apple Cornbread* or *Caramel Corn,* to name a few. You will find a tempting recipe for every occasion in this collection. Includes corn facts and trivia too!

5 1/2 x 8 1/2 — 88 pages . . . $6.95

APPLE LOVERS COOK BOOK

Celebrating America's favorite—the apple! 150 recipes for main and side dishes, appetizers, salads, breads, muffins, cakes, pies, desserts, beverages, and preserves, all kitchen-tested by Shirley Munson and Jo Nelson.

5 1/2 x 8 1/2 — 120 Pages . . . $6.95

BERRY LOVERS COOK BOOK

Berrylicious recipes for enjoying these natural wonders. From *Blueberry Muffins, Strawberry Cheesecake* and *Raspberry Sticky Rolls* to *Boysenberry Mint Frosty* or *Gooseberry Crunch,* you will find tasty recipes that will bring raves from your friends and family. Includes berry facts and trivia.

5 1/2 x 8 1/2 — 96 Pages . . . $6.95

THE JOY OF MUFFINS
The International Muffin Cook Book

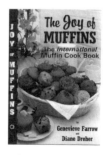

Recipes for German Streusel, Finnish Cranberry, Italian Amaretto, Greek Baklava, Chinese Almond, Jamaican Banana, Swiss Fondue, microwave section and ten recipes for oat bran muffins . . . 50 recipes in all! By Genevieve Farrow and Diane Dreher.

5 1/2 x 8 1/2 — 120 Pages . . . $5.95

VEGGIE LOVERS COOK BOOK

Everyone will love these no-cholesterol, no-animal recipes! Over 200 nutritious, flavorful recipes by Chef Morty Star. Includes a foreword by Dr. Michael Klaper. Nutritional analysis for each recipe to help you plan a healthy diet.

5 1/2 x 8 1/2 — 128 pages . . . $6.95

GOLDEN WEST PUBLISHERS

 4113 N. Longview Ave. • Phoenix, AZ 85014

www.goldenwestpublishers.com • **1-800-658-5830** • FAX 602-279-6901

Qty	Title	Price	Amount
	Apple Lovers Cook Book	**6.95**	
	Bean Lovers Cook Book	**6.95**	
	Berry Lovers Cook Book	**6.95**	
	Best Barbecue Recipes	**5.95**	
	Chili-Lovers' Cook Book	**5.95**	
	Chip and Dip Lovers Cook Book	**5.95**	
	Citrus Lovers Cook Book	**6.95**	
	Colorado Cook Book	**6.95**	
	Corn Lovers Cook Book	**6.95**	
	Illinois Cook Book	**6.95**	
	Iowa Cook Book	**6.95**	
	Kansas Cook Book	**6.95**	
	Joy of Muffins	**5.95**	
	Oklahoma Cook Book	**6.95**	
	Pecan Lovers Cook Book	**6.95**	
	Pumpkin Lovers Cook Book	**6.95**	
	Salsa Lovers Cook Book	**5.95**	
	Texas Cook Book	**6.95**	
	Tortilla Lovers Cook Book	**6.95**	
	Veggie Lovers Cook Book	**6.95**	
Shipping & Handling Add ⟶	U.S. & Canada	$3.00	
	Other countries	$5.00	

☐ My Check or Money Order Enclosed $ _____

☐ MasterCard   ☐ VISA   ($20 credit card minimum)

(Payable in U.S. funds)

Acct. No.	Exp. Date
Signature	
Name	Telephone
Address	
City/State/Zip	**Call for a FREE catalog of all of our titles** Kansas CkBk
7/00	

This order blank may be photo-copied.